The Ultimate Checklist for Life

Presented To:

_____

Presented By:

_____

Date:

_____

The Ultimate
Checklist for Life

The Ultimate Checklist for Life

THOMAS NELSON
Since 1798

NASHVILLE   DALLAS   MEXICO CITY   RIO DE JANEIRO   BEIJING

The Ultimate Checklist for Life © 2007 by Thomas Nelson, Inc.

This book was compiled from the following books in the *Checklist for Life* series:
Checklist for Life (manuscript written and prepared by Steve Parolini)
Checklist for Life for Women (manuscript written and prepared by Candi Paull)
Checklist for Life for Men (manuscript written by Todd Hafer, Mark Moesta, Mark Weising, and Kyle Olund in conjunction with Snapdragon Editorial Group, Inc.)
Checklist for Life for Teens (manuscript written and prepared by Marcia Ford)
Checklist for Life for Moms (manuscript written and prepared by Sarah M. Hupp, with contributions from Mary Tucker)
Checklist for Life for Leaders (manuscript written and prepared by Marcia Ford and Angie Kiesling)
Checklist for Life for Graduates (manuscript written by Marcia Ford)
Checklist for Life for Teachers (manuscript written and prepared by Marcia Ford)

Published in Nashville, Tennessee, by Thomas Nelson. Thomas Nelson is a trademark of Thomas Nelson, Inc.

Thomas Nelson, Inc. titles may be purchased in bulk for educational, business, fund-raising, or sales promotional use. For information, please e-mail SpecialMarkets@ThomasNelson.com.

Scripture quotations noted NKJV are from THE NEW KING JAMES VERSION. © 1979, 1980, 1982, Thomas Nelson, Inc., Publishers.

See page 336 for all Scripture translations used in this collection.

Original Series Design: Whisner Design Group

ISBN 978-1-4041-1365-7

Printed in the United States of America

07 08 09 10 11 QW 5 4 3 2 1

Heart Attitude

I will be confident that God knows my heart.

Table of Contents

Table of Contents Continued

Table of Contents Continued

Introduction

Give me understanding, and I shall live. —PSALM 119:144 NKJV

Are you prepared for life?

Life is a journey that can often lead you to unexpected places. It's an adventure with a penchant for hurling challenges and opportunities in your path. Are you equipped for the challenges? Geared up to seize the opportunities?

As any great adventurer will tell you, it's advisable to bring along the right tools when you set out on a journey. If your journey is a search for a fulfilling and confident life, *The Ultimate Checklist for Life* may be just the tool set you're looking for. Whether you're in the middle of a difficult challenge today or simply preparing for the ones that will come tomorrow, this book can help you know which fork in the road you should take. When opportunities arise, it can help you make the most of your circumstances.

The seventy-six overviews or insight passages in this how-to guide explore a wide variety of topics—from fighting fear, to knowing God's forgiveness, to setting and reaching goals. Want to be prepared for many of life's surprises? Read the book cover to cover. Dealing with a specific challenge or opportunity? Look up the topic in the Table of Contents and study that meditation.

Immerse yourself in and anchor your life to the timeless wisdom and truth of God's Word. Explore the sensible strategies that can help you take confident steps in your life journey. Then complete the checklists. The *I Will* checklists guide you in reflecting on the topic and embracing the wisdom that can help you make the most of your challenge or opportunity. The *Things to Do* checklists provide practical ideas for applying this wisdom to your life today.

With entries from all of the popular books in the *Checklist for Life* series, *The Ultimate Checklist for Life* is a field guide to life's incredible journey. Keep it with you and be prepared for a great life!

Life is God's novel. Let him write it. —ISAAC BASHEVIS SINGER

Trust in the LORD, and do good; dwell in the land, and feed on His faithfulness.

PSALM 37:3 NKJV

Call on God, but row away from the rocks.

RALPH WALDO EMERSON

What is faith? It is the confident assurance that what we hope for is going to happen. It is the evidence of things we cannot yet see.

HEBREWS 11:1 THE MESSAGE

The way from God to a human heart is through a human heart.

SAMUEL GORDON

The fruit of the Spirit is love, joy, peace, longsuffering, kindness, goodness, faithfulness, gentleness, self-control. Against such there is no law.

GALATIANS 5:22–23 NKJV

Aim at Heaven and you will get earth "thrown in": aim at earth and you will get neither.

C. S. LEWIS

The two most powerful warriors are patience and time.
—LEO TOLSTOY

The first duty of love is to listen.
—PAUL TILLICH

Checklist for Life

*Courage is almost a contradiction in terms. It means a
strong desire to live taking the form of a readiness to die.*
        —G. K. Chesterton

*Let nothing be done through selfish ambition or conceit,
but in lowliness of mind let each esteem others better than
himself.*
        —Philippians 2:3 NKJV

Frequent Flyer Meals

They continued steadfastly in the apostles' doctrine and fellowship, in the breaking of bread, and in prayers.

—*Acts 2:42* NKJV

For an hour or two each week, millions of people participate in church services around the world. Before the services begin, congregation members smile and nod at one another, shake hands, and may even ask, "How are you doing?" When the services are over, they smile and nod again, shake hands, and say, "See you next week" before heading off in separate directions. To these people, church is a weekly activity that only rarely intersects with regular life.

In the days of the early church, there was little if any distinction between church and regular life. That's because church wasn't a place to go; rather, it was the people with whom you associated in your desire to grow in faith. The early church did this in small groups. They didn't gather just once a week; they gathered and fellowshipped every day and in all aspects of their lives. Descriptions of the early church like the ones found in the book of Acts frequently include the mention of "breaking bread." Breaking bread represented the concept of fellowship, of doing life together.

This idea is just as applicable today. The idea of doing life together is quite simple. It means exploring and applying your faith in community with others. The best way to do this is in a small group (eight to twelve people is just about right). Use your time together to get to know everyone. Share dreams. Tell memories. Study the Bible. Pray. As you get to know each other, celebrate each person's successes. Throw birthday parties or congratulations-on-a-new-job parties. Serve each other's needs in practical ways. Pick up the children of a group member from school or offer a helping hand when a group member is experiencing lean financial times. Most of all, learn to love one another.

If this kind of small group is not available, there are other ways of doing life with your church community. Explore the possibilities of small ministries within the larger ministry of your local church. Consider sharing community with members of your choir, your altar guild, your men's fellowship, your Bible study group, your needleworkers guild, your grounds committee, your church's supper club. The opportunities for living your fellowship by the example of the early church are still available and just as valuable today.

In the time you spend with members of your small group, you will discover what it means to do life together. You will get a glimpse of the reason God created you in the first place—to do life with Him.

I Will

Look for opportunities to share life experiences with friends.

yes   _no_

Know that time spent with friends is a key to growing closer together.

yes   _no_

Seek to integrate church life with real life in my relationships.

yes   _no_

Understand that there is some risk involved in doing life with others.

yes   _no_

Desire to grow closer to friends.

yes   _no_

Examine my current relationships and see if I can break bread more often with friends.

yes   _no_

Things to Do

☐ _Plan a get-together with a few friends and talk about what it means to do life together._

☐ _Throw a celebration for those you wish to know better._

☐ _Choose one or two new people you'd like to know better and invite them to dinner._

☐ _Make a list of practical ways to serve people you do life with and then commit to those actions._

☐ _Spend a weekend helping a friend with tasks such as cleaning house, doing laundry, and washing dishes._

☐ _Invite members of your small group to a movie, play, concert, or other nonchurch event._

Things to Remember

All of you be of one mind, having compassion for one another; love as brothers, be tenderhearted, be courteous.

1 PETER 3:8 NKJV

We took sweet counsel together, and walked to the house of God in the throng.

PSALM 55:14 NKJV

Can two walk together, unless they are agreed?

AMOS 3:3 NKJV

Comfort one another.

1 THESSALONIANS 4:18 NKJV

Bear one another's burdens, and in this way you will fulfill the law of Christ.

GALATIANS 6:2 NRSV

All who believed were together, and had all things in common.

ACTS 2:42 NKJV

Paul wrote: I hope to see you on my journey, and to be helped on my way there by you, if first I may enjoy your company for a while.

ROMANS 15:24 NKJV

To live in prayer together is to walk in love together.

—MARGARET MOORE JACOBS

God calls us not to solitary sainthood but to fellowship in a company of committed men.

—DAVID SCHULLER

God's Provision

What You Really Need

Jesus said, "Do not seek what you should eat or what you should drink, nor have an anxious mind. . . . Seek the kingdom of God, and all these things shall be added to you."

—*Luke 12:29, 31* NKJV

The list of needs that people claim has been steadily rising over the past fifty years or so. A list that used to consist of little more than essentials such as food, water, clothing, and shelter has been expanded in recent time to include everything from specific kinds of food (no beets, please) to a computer and Internet hookup. In a world driven by the pursuit of more and more wants masquerading as needs, it's getting harder to sift through such a list and uncover the true necessities.

Go ahead and try. Pare back your own list until it's purely the needs. Once you've done this, however, Jesus has a surprising message for you: Stop pursuing items on this list too. Seek instead to grow your relationship with God.

Jesus' message is more than a challenge, however. It is a promise. Seek to know God and He'll take care of your needs and sustain you.

The key to trusting God for your needs begins with the understanding that Jesus' message is really all about priorities. An important step in this process is to be deliberate about your relationship with God. Don't assume that regular church attendance and Bible study are going to automatically make God a priority. Pray often. Invite God daily to reveal Himself to you. Ask God to direct your day—your decisions, the words you speak, even your thoughts. Enter each day anticipating new insight into God's will for your life.

Then be thankful. Make a quick mental list of what God has already provided in your life. Even if you consider your circumstances to be meager, your list is bound to be long. A thankful heart can help keep God at the top of your list.

Shrink your worry list. Examine areas in your life where anxiety rules. Does your worrying really make a positive difference in those situations? If not, dump the worry.

Finally, be diligent in whatever is your chosen profession. Trusting in God's provision doesn't mean quitting your job and sitting in a field with outstretched hands. God provides opportunities as well as specific needs. Those opportunities may indeed be God's way of clothing or feeding you.

The closer you grow to God, the more you'll begin to see the many ways in which He provides—and the more you'll be willing to trust Him for that provision.

I Will

Order my priorities to focus on my relationship with God first.	*yes*	*no*
Trust God to provide for my needs.	*yes*	*no*
Consider the real needs I have.	*yes*	*no*
Know that my needs are different than wants.	*yes*	*no*
Seek to grow closer to God every day.	*yes*	*no*
Be thankful for all God has already provided.	*yes*	*no*
Reduce the number of worries I currently have.	*yes*	*no*

Things to Do

☐ *Make a list of the actual needs you have.*

☐ *Ask God for the ability to trust in His provision.*

☐ *Read Jesus' Sermon on the Mount (Matthew 5–7) and consider the implications for how I approach wants and needs in life.*

☐ *Ask a pastor or other church leader for new ideas on how to seek God's kingdom.*

☐ *Write a thank-you note to God listing the ways in which He has provided for your needs.*

☐ *Surf the Internet for articles on a missionary (perhaps Jim Elliot or Hudson Taylor) and see what you can learn about trusting in God's provision.*

Things to Remember

We know that all things work together for good to those who love God, to those who are the called according to His purpose.

ROMANS 8:28 NKJV

Jesus said to them, "What kind of conversation is this that you have with one another as you walk and are sad?"

LUKE 24:17 NKJV

Though the fig tree may not blossom, nor fruit be on the vines; though the labor of the olive may fail, and the fields yield no food; though the flock may be cut off from the fold, and there be no herd in the stalls—yet I will rejoice in the LORD, I will joy in the God of my salvation.

HABAKKUK 3:17–18 NKJV

Humble yourselves under the mighty hand of God, that He may exalt you in due time.

1 PETER 5:6–7 NKJV

Commit everything you do to the LORD. Trust him, and he will help you.

PSALM 37:5 NLT

Disappointment, when it involves neither shame nor loss, is as good as success, for it supplies as many images to the mind, and as many topics to the tongue.

—SAMUEL JOHNSON

Why art thou disquieted; because it happeneth not to thee according to thy wishes and desires? Who is he that hath everything according to his will? Neither I, nor thou, nor any man upon the earth.

—THOMAS À KEMPIS

When You Don't Get What You Deserve

It is God who saved us and chose us to live a holy life. He did this not because we deserved it, but because that was his plan long before the world began—to show his love and kindness to us through Christ Jesus.

—*2 Timothy 1:9* NKJV

One of the more enduring of the McDonald's commercial jingles made this rather bold pronouncement: "You deserve a break today." Did millions of Americans really deserve a break? Well, a busy life with no time to rest certainly sounds like a good reason to take a break. But did the people really deserve a break? Though McDonald's may have used the concept of deservedness in a lighthearted way, it triggers the thought-provoking question, What do people really deserve?

If you examine the history of humanity as recorded in the Bible, there is no question about what people deserve. People messed up. By their own free will, they chose to disobey God and they ushered sin into the world. Because of sin, all of humanity deserves to be eternally separated from God. But God had a different idea. Through the gift of his son's life, He chose to save people from sin. He gave people the very thing they didn't deserve—the possibility of new life and an eternity by His side in heaven. This is the definition of grace.

The path to receiving grace is clearly marked in Scripture. When you choose to follow Christ and accept forgiveness, grace is yours. Instead of a Christ-less eternity, you are given eternal life. There is no cost—else it wouldn't be grace but something you had to work for.

Grace requires no further action on your part. You've been saved from destruction. But there are some natural responses to this grace that spring forth upon its acceptance. Will you lose your place in heaven if you don't respond in this way? No. And you won't lose it when you sin again—and you will. God's grace is big enough to handle your mistakes. Still, consider the following ways you might respond to this incredible gift from God.

Take advantage of every opportunity to become a fully devoted Christ-follower. If you don't already have a home church—seek one out that will challenge you to grow and encourage you along the way.

Pray often. Ask God for insight into His will for your life. Read the Bible to learn more about God and about what it means to follow God. Join a Bible study group and dig deeper into the Scriptures to find practical applications for your daily life.

Grace is free. Reflect on this gift that you don't deserve or take a backward glance at what you do deserve. Is there any more compelling reason to seek a closer relationship with God?

I Will

Thank God for the gift of grace.   *yes*   *no*

Consider how I should respond to God's grace.   *yes*   *no*

Seek to become a fully devoted Christ-follower.   *yes*   *no*

Examine my heart to see how I have responded to
God's gift of grace.   *yes*   *no*

Know that God's gift of grace can't be purchased
through good works.   *yes*   *no*

Be thankful that the gift of grace doesn't go away
when I sin.   *yes*   *no*

Things to Do

☐ Ask God to give you wisdom to know the right response to His gift of grace.

☐ Write a poem or song to God thanking Him for grace.

☐ Look up the word grace in a dictionary and compare the definition to your definition of God's grace.

☐ Find a copy of the Newsboys' song "Real Good Thing" and listen to it (it's on their Going Public CD).

☐ Ask a church friend or pastor to share their understanding of God's grace.

☐ Create a Because of Grace journal where you can list steps you take in response to God's grace. Write your first entries right away.

Things to Remember

If by grace, then it is no longer of works;
otherwise grace is no longer grace. But if
it is of works, it is no longer grace;
otherwise work is no longer work.

ROMANS 11:6 NKJV

The law was given through Moses, but
grace and truth came through Jesus
Christ.

JOHN 1:17 NKJV

Prepare your minds for service and have
self-control. All your hope should be for
the gift of grace that will be yours when
Jesus Christ is shown to you.

1 PETER 1:13 NCV

We believe that through the grace of the
Lord Jesus Christ we shall be saved in
the same manner as they.

ACTS 15:11 NKJV

God is able to make all grace abound
toward you, that you, always having all
sufficiency in all things, may have an
abundance for every good work.

2 CORINTHIANS 9:8 NKJV

God gave that grace to us freely, in
Christ, the One he loves.

EPHESIANS 1:6 NCV

Grace is not sought
nor bought nor
wrought. It is a
free gift of
Almighty God to
needy mankind.

—BILLY GRAHAM

All men who live
with any degree of
serenity live by
some assurance of
grace.

—REINHOLD NIEBUHR

Wind Chasing

I looked on all the works that my hands had done and on the labor in which I had toiled; and indeed all was vanity and grasping for the wind. There was no profit under the sun.

—*Ecclesiastes 2:11* NKJV

In the lifelong search for meaning, you may endure seasons when life seems to have no point. All your great deeds—your accomplishments at work, your success in relationships—suddenly seem like puffs of smoke. They're here for a moment, then gone. The author of Ecclesiastes must have had a moment like that when he wrote, "All was vanity and grasping for the wind."

The writer of the Kansas song "Dust in the Wind" may have had a similar transcendent moment. The band's song was an instant hit with the public, quite possibly because so many people could relate to its groping-for-the-meaning-of-life lyrics. In moments like this, you realize you are here merely for a blip of time in the context of eternity. Your accomplishments, no matter how great among people, mean little or nothing in the broader scope of things. You are but dust in the wind, but only—and this is critical—when you look for your self-worth in earthly tasks and earthly relationships.

All people are created with a God-shaped hole that's waiting to be filled. When you try to fill that hole with anything other than God, such as worldly success or conquests, life never quite finds its purpose. Left unfilled, that God-shaped hole leaves a feeling of emptiness that comes and goes at will.

When you begin a relationship with God, life finds a purpose. Life begins to make sense, and the emptiness disappears. It's important to understand that just about everyone goes through the wilderness times. You're not alone when you feel empty inside.

Even when you come to know God, you may still find yourself feeling alone or lost at times. That doesn't mean God has left you. It may simply mean you have lost sight of God. When you have these moments, open the Bible. Read Ecclesiastes to remind yourself that you're not alone in your search for significance. Read Psalms to rediscover a range of experience in what it means to be in relationship with God. Then read the Gospel of John to see just how much Jesus loves you.

You may find yourself still struggling to know what your purpose is in life. A life's purpose may include some grand task, but it may also be in the details. Make it your life's work to grow closer to God and you'll uncover those details along the way.

I Will

Examine what it means to have a "God-shaped hole."

yes   _no_

Understand that a relationship with God gives life purpose.

yes   _no_

Be comforted to know that I am not alone in feeling lost or purposeless at times.

yes   _no_

Seek out God through the Bible when I have a hard time discovering meaning.

yes   _no_

Know that it's not unusual at times to feel like life has no purpose.

yes   _no_

Consider that my purpose in life may not be a single task but the way in which I live.

yes   _no_

Things to Do

☐ _Read the entire book of Ecclesiastes and reflect on the author's examination of the difference between life without God and life centered on God._

☐ _Ask God to help you see the real meaning of life in practical ways._

☐ _Listen to the song "Dust in the Wind" and consider what its message says about the purpose of life._

☐ _Interview five people at random and ask the question, "Where do you find your significance in life?"_

☐ _Think of three ways in which God has used you to have an impact on the lives of others._

Things to Remember

Whatever is born of God overcomes the world. And this is the victory that has overcome the world—our faith.

1 JOHN 5:4 NKJV

There is no condemnation for those who belong to Christ Jesus.

ROMANS 8:1 NKJV

In all these things we are more than conquerors through Him who loved us.

ROMANS 8:37 NKJV

God has given me the wonderful privilege of telling everyone about this plan of his; and he has given me his power and special ability to do it well.

EPHESIANS 3:7 TLB

Who knows what is good for man in life, all the days of his vain life which he passes like a shadow? Who can tell a man what will happen after him under the sun?

ECCLESIASTES 6:12 NKJV

Jesus said, "Most assuredly, I say to you, he who believes in Me, the works that I do he will do also; and greater works than these he will do, because I go to My Father."

JOHN 14:12 NKJV

Life is filled with meaning as soon as Jesus Christ enters into it.

—STEPHEN NEILL

Living a good, decent, Christian life is what's important; live that life and the rest will follow.

—SPIKE MILLIGAN

Arms That Circle the Universe

Jesus said, "God so loved the world, that he gave his only begotten Son, that whosoever believeth in him should not perish, but have everlasting life."

—John 3:16 KJV

Think big, really big. This evening, glance outside at the homes and buildings in your neighborhood. Then look to the horizon and the lights that betray the breadth of your town or city. Look at the night sky. Use your imagination to see beyond the solar system, the Milky Way galaxy, and even farther—to the stars that no one has even seen yet. Now draw a box around all you can imagine.

God's love is bigger. But a love so big is incomprehensible. So God chose to show His love in a way that humanity might understand: He sent His Son, Jesus, to die on the cross so that people could have everlasting life.

The concept of sacrifice is foreign to many people. Some might think that handing the remote control to a spouse or child is a sacrifice. Others might see giving up a favorite food as a sacrifice. But real sacrifice costs much more than a moment of inconvenience.

In Old Testament times, the Israelites sacrificed animals to honor God. But as humanity stumbled and slipped farther and farther away from God, the sacrifices meant less and less. Sin ruled and separated God from people. In God's great plan, there was only one way to bring the people back to Him: the ultimate sacrifice of His own Son.

Because of God's great love for humanity, Jesus died on the cross. But Jesus didn't just die, He defeated death and opened up a path to the Father once again. God's love is big enough to circle the universe and small enough to be focused just on you.

God's love is a personal love. He wants to have a unique relationship with you. When you pray, ask God to reveal Himself to you. Simply say, "I want to know You." Then allow space in your life for God to speak to you through His Spirit. When you study the Bible, imagine it was written just for you. Study the way God acts in Scripture. Get to know His characteristics. Look for the many different ways God shows love to His people.

God's love is eternal. It doesn't go away when you turn your back on God. It doesn't fluctuate according to your love for Him. It is a constant, abiding love.

God's love is always near, and it includes a promise for those who love Him—the promise of everlasting life.

I Will

Know that God's love is beyond compare.

yes _no_

Understand that God's love prompted Him to send
Jesus to die for my sins.

yes _no_

Be thankful that God loved me enough to give me
a new chance to know Him.

yes _no_

Recognize that God's love is a personal love.

yes _no_

Realize that God's love is eternal.

yes _no_

Accept that God's love will always be near.

yes _no_

Look for ways to express my gratitude
for God's love.

yes _no_

Things to Do

☐ _Thank God for loving you enough to sacrifice His son and build a bridge back to God._

☐ _Write a poem describing how you feel about God's love._

☐ _Make a list of human characteristics of love and then compare these to your understanding of God's love._

☐ _Look at a book on astronomy and attempt to grasp the "bigness" of the universe. Then consider what it means that God's love is more amazing than the size of the universe._

☐ _Talk with a Christian friend about how you can show thanks to God for His love._

☐ _Sing along with a gospel CD praising God's great love._

Things to Remember

He who does not love does not know God, for God is love.

1 JOHN 4:8 NKJV

We know how much God loves us, and we have put our trust in Him. God is love, and all who live in love live in God, and God lives in them.

1 JOHN 4:16 NKJV

The LORD has appeared of old to me, saying: "Yes, I have loved you with an everlasting love; therefore with lovingkindness I have drawn you."

JEREMIAH 31:3 NKJV

Hope does not disappoint, because the love of God has been poured out in our hearts by the Holy Spirit who was given to us.

ROMANS 5:5 NKJV

May the Lord direct your hearts into the love of God and into the patience of Christ.

2 THESSALONIANS 3:5 NKJV

God our Savior showed us his kindness and love.

TITUS 3:4 NLT

God does not love us because we are valuable. We are valuable because God loves us.

—FULTON J. SHEEN

If God takes your lump of clay and remolds it, it will be on the basis of love and not on the basis of power over you.

—JAMES CONWAY

Out of Time

This is the promise that He has promised us—eternal life.

—1 John 2:25 NKJV

Do a Web search on the word *eternal* and you'll come up with more than a million hits, referencing everything from the song "Eternal Flame" by the Bangles to vampires to video games, along with a multitude of religious and quasi-religious sites. The same word is used casually in advertising too. Wouldn't you like to enjoy eternal youth simply by applying some fancy cream from a little jar?

The concept of *eternity* comes, of course, from the only Person who's known what it looks like: God. It is a word that literally means "for all time." But despite the fact that eternal life is God's alone to give, people continue to search for a way to hang on to one more day of life on earth through health, mysticism, and even religion.

God has said quite plainly that you can't do a thing to add to your days here on earth (Psalm 39:4). They are numbered. However, He also promises the brass ring of eternity for all who follow Him. The fountain of youth may be fiction, but the possibility of living forever is not.

How can you get a handle on something that is so far beyond earthly, time-bound understanding? You can't, at least not fully. But you can know that eternal life is a promise.

It is possible to get so caught up by the promise of eternal life that today might seem almost meaningless. But that's not the point of God's promise. Eternal life is a gift for those who follow God, but it isn't something to rush off to. God desires that you first live your life fully on earth. Get to know God today. Delve into God's Word and seek understanding of God's will. Then, when your days are up, you get the prize of eternal life.

You may be wondering what eternal life might look like. Though the Bible's depiction of heaven includes clues to life after death, the human mind simply can't paint a clear picture of "forever."

You can enjoy the hope of eternity today. That hope can fuel those difficult days you're going to experience while still on earth. It can diminish the pain and suffering you experience by helping you see an eternal perspective. And it can motivate you to make choices that will matter in eternity—focusing on making a difference in the lives of others instead of storing up worldly goods.

I Will

Realize that eternity is something only God fully understands.

yes   _no_

Know that I can't add a day to my life here on earth.

yes   _no_

Understand that the promise of eternal life is for those who follow God.

yes   _no_

Be thankful for the gift of eternal life.

yes   _no_

Not focus on eternity so much that I forget to live my life today.

yes   _no_

Recognize that I can't paint an accurate picture of eternal life.

yes   _no_

Things to Do

☐ _Ask God to reveal how the hope of eternal life ought to influence your daily decisions._

☐ _Interview five or ten children in a Sunday school class about what eternal life means to them and then compare their answers to your beliefs on eternal life._

☐ _Do your own Web search on the word_ eternal. _See what you can learn about what people believe lasts forever._

☐ _Make a list of actions that have a positive 7 significance and choose to do some of these._

☐ _Draw or paint an abstract picture representing your feelings about eternal life._

Things to Remember

A certain ruler asked Him, saying, "Good Teacher, what shall I do to inherit eternal life?"

LUKE 18:18 NKJV

Many of those who sleep in the dust of the earth shall awake, some to everlasting life, some to shame and everlasting contempt.

DANIEL 12:2 NKJV

Jesus said, "No one who drinks the water I give will ever be thirsty again. The water I give is like a flowing fountain that gives eternal life."

JOHN 4:14 CEV

Jesus said, "This is the way to have eternal life—to know you, the only true God, and Jesus Christ, the one you sent to earth."

JOHN 17:3 NLT

He will give eternal life to those who patiently do the will of God, seeking for the unseen glory and honor and eternal life that he offers.

ROMANS 2:7 TLB

Here in this world He bids us come, there in the next He shall bid us welcome.

—JOHN DONNE

Surely God would not have created such a being as man . . . to exist only for a day! No, no, man was made for immortality.

—ABRAHAM LINCOLN

Mysterious Ways

Oh, the depth of the riches both of the wisdom and knowledge of God! How unsearchable are His judgments and His ways past finding out!

—Romans 11:33 NKJV

People are fascinated by mystery. A quick flip through the local TV listings is proof enough of that. You'll find everything from traditional whodunits to more obscure fare such as shows exploring the possibility of aliens or examining the latest conspiracy theories. The lure of the unknown is strong. People are drawn to mystery in part because they want to solve it, but equally because they want to know there is no plausible answer.

Attempting to comprehend God is like trying to get the answers to all your other mystery questions at the same time. Who else but the only Person who has lived for eternity would understand infinity? Who else but the One who created the universe would know how big it is?

With the limitations of a human mind, you can't fully understand God. Paul was intimately aware of this when he wrote about the depth of God's wisdom in Romans. But that didn't stop Paul from trying to know God. And that is precisely what God desires for you—that you get to know Him.

Because God is relational, you can get to know Him simply by talking with Him. Your knowledge of God will grow according to how much time you spend with Him in prayer. As you learn how God answers prayer, you'll come to know His thoughts. You'll learn what is important to God. And you'll discover that God's ways are not always knowable.

You can also know God by observing His creation. By studying the stars you can see His greatness; by watching an elephant, His creativity. His greatest creation, people, can teach you much about God—keep in mind that people were created in God's image. Like you, God desires companionship (that is why He created people in the first place). Like you, God desires to be loved without condition (that is why He gave you free will).

Perhaps the best way to know God is to read His résumé: the Bible. Through the stories and wisdom presented in God's Word, you can learn about God's unending love. You can uncover insights into God's character—that He is merciful, just, patient, powerful, all-knowing. There is no end to the amount of truth you can uncover about God by reading the Bible.

Be compelled by the mystery of God to seek Him even more diligently.

I Will

Recognize that God is a God of mystery.　　　yes　　no

Realize that God wants me to know Him.　　　yes　　no

Accept that I can't fully know God.　　　yes　　no

Get to know God through regular prayer.　　　yes　　no

See God in His creation—particularly through
relationships with other people.　　　yes　　no

Read the Bible often to better know God.　　　yes　　no

Be diligent about getting to know God.　　　yes　　no

Things to Do

☐ *Determine what you consider to be the three greatest mysteries about God or His creation.*

☐ *Watch a mystery on television and compare the characters' desire to solve the mystery with your desire to understand God.*

☐ *Talk with a friend about what excites you most and frustrates you most about the mystery of God.*

☐ *Use a calendar to schedule your Bible-reading times for the next week so you can get to know God better.*

☐ *Write down your thoughts about how the following quotation from Albert Einstein relates to your relationship with God: "The most beautiful experience we can have is the mysterious."*

Things to Remember

Therefore You are great, O Lord GOD.
For there is none like You, nor is there
any God besides You, according to all
that we have heard with our ears.

2 SAMUEL 7:22 NKJV

No one has seen God at any time. The
only begotten Son, who is in the bosom
of the Father, He has declared Him.

JOHN 1:18 NKJV

God is not a man, that He should lie,
nor a son of man, that He should
repent. Has He said, and will He not do?
Or has He spoken, and will He not
make it good?

NUMBERS 23:19 NKJV

Solomon said, "Will God indeed dwell
on the earth? Behold, heaven and the
heaven of heavens cannot contain You.
How much less this temple which I have
built!"

1 KINGS 8:27 NKJV

If our heart condemns us, God is greater
than our heart, and knows all things.

1 JOHN 3:20 NKJV

Righteousness and justice are the
foundation of Your throne; mercy and
truth go before Your face.

PSALM 89:14 NKJV

His center is everywhere, His circumference is nowhere.

—HENRY LAW

As I read the Bible, I seem to find holiness to be His supreme attribute.

—BILLY GRAHAM

Checklist for Life *for* Women

Always be in a state of expectancy and see that you leave room for God to come in as He likes.
        —Oswald Chambers

We are His workmanship, created in Christ Jesus for good works, which God prepared beforehand that we should walk in them.
        —Ephesians 2:10 NKJV

Trusting God

Divine Appointments

Do not boast about tomorrow, for you do not know what a day will bring forth.

—PROVERBS 27:1 NIV

No matter how you plan and prepare, each day brings its own unexpected encounters. No matter how predictable and mundane your life may feel, surprises always wait around the corner. These are called divine appointments. A divine appointment may be a wonderful contact with a long-lost friend or an unexpected emergency that takes you to a hospital waiting room. You may meet a new person or lose a loved one. You may reach a long-desired goal or may have to put aside a cherished dream. There will always be many detours, disasters, and unexpected delights scattered along your path.

Sometimes divine encounters can be dramatic and surprising. When the angel came to Mary, she was afraid, but she said yes to God. Jesus confronted Paul on the road to Damascus, and Paul's entire life changed with that encounter. Philip met the Ethiopian eunuch on the road and ended up explaining the Scriptures to him and baptizing him. But not all divine appointments take place in unusual circumstances. God often brings people together in the course of their daily routine. Paul met Lydia when he went down to the river to where a regular prayer meeting was being held. Peter and John were on their way to afternoon prayer in the temple in Jerusalem when they met and healed a man crippled from birth. A casual encounter can have life-changing effects when God is at work through His people.

Keep in mind that though you may be unable to change a situation, you still have control over how you will respond. When your plans are interrupted, take a deep breath and give yourself time to think before you react. Take care of the need that is confronting you at the moment. Look at each person who needs something from you as if he or she is sent from God. Say a quick prayer and ask God to guide you and give you patience and wisdom. Trust the process and be open to God's leading through the unexpected.

Realize that each encounter is a divine appointment, each problem another opportunity for God to show you His faithfulness. When a difficult situation arises, will you choose to rest in Him? When a desired outcome is delayed, are you willing to listen for the lesson in the detour? Are you willing to receive the unexpected gifts a day brings and be open to divine appointments?

I Will

Understand that I am finite and that God will take care of the things that are beyond my control.
_____ yes   _____ no

Receive the unexpected gifts a day brings.
_____ yes   _____ no

Listen for God's wisdom in every situation.
_____ yes   _____ no

Look for the lesson in each detour, delay, and unexpected delight.
_____ yes   _____ no

Be flexible when the unexpected enters my day.
_____ yes   _____ no

Remember that God works all things together for good for those who love Him.
_____ yes   _____ no

Look at each person I encounter as someone God has sent into my life.
_____ yes   _____ no

Things to Do

☐ Set aside five minutes to pray for God's guidance about a specific situation that troubles you.

☐ Introduce yourself to a new person at church.

☐ Memorize a Bible verse to remind yourself that your life is in God's hands (perhaps Psalm 46:1).

☐ Take a break in the middle of your busy day to rest, reflect, and regain perspective.

☐ Look in the mirror and see yourself as someone God loves.

☐ Go to a crowded shopping mall, watch all the different people, and think about how much God loves each person you see.

Things to Remember

The LORD performs wonders that cannot be fathomed, miracles that cannot be counted.

JOB 5:9 NIV

I saw that there is nothing better than that all should enjoy their work, for that is their lot; who can bring them to see what will be after them?

ECCLESIASTES 3:22 NRSV

God sees that justice is done, and he watches over everyone who is faithful to him.

PROVERBS 2:8 CEV

Why, you do not even know what will happen tomorrow. What is your life? You are a mist that appears for a little while and then vanishes. Instead, you ought to say, "If it is the Lord's will, we will live and do this or that."

JAMES 4:14–15 NIV

Trust in the LORD with all your heart, and lean not on your own understanding: In all your ways acknowledge Him, and He shall direct your paths.

PROVERBS 3:5–6 NKJV

Faith is not belief without proof, but trust without reservations.

—ELTON TRUEBLOOD

O Lord, thou knowest that which is best for us. Let this or that be done, as thou shalt please. Give what thou wilt, how much thou wilt, and when thou wilt.

—THOMAS À KEMPIS

Strength

Inner Power

They go from strength to strength; each one appears before God in Zion.

—PSALM 84:7 NKJV

What is a woman of strength? Many examples of strong women are found in the Bible: Deborah, Esther, Phoebe, Sarah, and Mary, to name just a few. All these women had one thing in common. They had an inner strength that came from their relationship with God. They were strong without being obnoxious or domineering, free to use their gifts and talents to serve others in a loving partnership with God.

The Bible shows that all God's people are strong—and that all God's people are weak. You are strong in His strength and weak when you try to do everything in your own strength. Real strength does not ignore your weakness as a human being. You shouldn't be surprised when you experience weakness. It is part of the human condition to face weakness. God accepts you as you are, a mixture of strong and weak. He doesn't expect you to be Wonder Woman. But you can tap into an unfailing source of strength greater than mortal mind or muscular conditioning. You can be a woman of strength in God.

The Bible has plenty to say about strength during times of weakness. You may have high ideals, but many times the spirit is willing while the flesh is weak. Yet it is in times of weakness that your greatest strength may be found—the gentle strength of God's Spirit working in you. The word *Comforter* used in the New Testament literally means "with strength." Jesus promised His followers that "The Strengthener" would be with them forever.

God does not need women who are doormats. Nor does He want women to be dominators. You do not have to feign helplessness and weakness. Nor do you need to intimidate or denigrate others. Margaret Thatcher said, "Being powerful is like being a lady. If you have to tell people you are, you aren't." You can have a quiet strength that comes from knowing who you are in God. It is a gentle power that grows from strength of character, wisdom, and purpose.

How can you be a woman of strength and power today? You can honor your body by taking care of it so that you can maintain physical strength and fitness. You can honor your heart by standing for your beliefs and not giving up when times get tough. You can honor your relationship with God by using your gifts and abilities to make a better world for your family and community.

I Will

Understand that all true strength comes from God.

    yes   *no*

Have the strength to be kind, compassionate, and faithful.

    yes   *no*

Choose to live in God's strength by faith.

    yes   *no*

Stand for what I believe even when I face resistance.

    yes   *no*

Work with my natural strengths, offering my gifts and talents for the greater good of all.

    yes   *no*

Remember that being a servant reflects the hidden strength of God's love.

    yes   *no*

Understand that when I am weak, God can be strong for me.

    yes   *no*

Things to Do

☐ Give some time to a charitable organization or ministry that helps those who cannot help themselves.

☐ Take a class or seminar to learn a new skill or enhance a strength or talent.

☐ Enhance your exercise routine with some form of strength training.

☐ Read a book about the lives of strong women—from women in the Bible to heroines of the faith to modern women who accomplish great things.

☐ Make a list of your strengths and weaknesses.

☐ Examine your beliefs about femininity and strength and write about it in your journal.

Things to Remember

She girds herself with strength, and strengthens her arms.

PROVERBS 31:17 NKJV

The LORD said, "Do not fear, for I am with you; do not be dismayed, for I am your God. I will strengthen you and help you; I will uphold you with my righteous right hand."

ISAIAH 41:10 NIV

Be strong in the Lord and in the power of His might.

EPHESIANS 6:10 NKJV

Less is more and more is less. One righteous will outclass fifty wicked, for the wicked are moral weaklings but the righteous are God-strong.

PSALM 37:16–17 THE MESSAGE

I can do all things through Christ who strengthens me.

PHILIPPIANS 4:13 NKJV

As your days, so shall your strength be.

DEUTERONOMY 33:5 NKJV

Endurance develops strength of character in us.

ROMANS 5:4 NLT

Nothing is so strong as gentleness: nothing so gentle as real strength.

—SAINT FRANCIS DE SALES

Because of an emphasis on strong men, we sometimes overlook the mighty women in the Bible, but they are there: Priscilla, Phoebe, and Sarah. Or Miriam, Deborah, Huldah, Esther, and Abigail. These were not quiet retiring ladies who never let their thoughts be known. They did not wait to respond to action: they created the action.

—BARBARA COOK

Brains, Beauty, and Spiritual Balance

As a ring of gold in a swine's snout, so is a lovely woman who lacks discretion.

—PROVERBS 11:22 NKJV

Remember when you were a young teenager, wishing you could be beautiful and stylish? It was a gawky and awkward time as you sought to find your way through the maze of fashion magazines, peer pressure, and fantasies of Cinderella evenings where the ugly duckling turns into a beautiful swan. Eventually you realized that reality was not going to be as smooth and perfect as the pictures in a fashion magazine. Being beautiful meant more than just looking good on the outside.

There is absolutely nothing wrong with wanting to be drop-dead beautiful—or at least in making your outside package prettier. Perfume, a new dress, high heels, a fresh haircut—let's admit it, they're all fun and part of the femininity that God created for you to enjoy. But when it comes to real style, the heart and the mind, not the outward appearance, are what matter.

The greatest beauty secret has nothing to do with make-up or fashion. It is being a woman who delights in God. She is, as the psalmist said, like a tree that never withers because she has her roots firmly planted in God. Her vital relationship with God gives her the ability to look beyond the surface to the reality beneath. She looks for substance—a kind heart, a discerning mind, and a strong faith—instead of being distracted by outward appearance. She knows that all good things come from God, but that some things are better than others. The heart that seeks after God is the most beautiful thing in the world.

A woman of style and substance is gracious and kind to all she meets. She lives her life from the heart, not from the ego. She notices the people that others miss and never takes a service or kindness for granted. Instead of whining about her troubles or complaining about others, she looks for the best in people and situations. She's savvy enough to know that people can let her down, but compassionate enough to understand why they do. She has learned compassion and wisdom and is able to see God's goodness in others. She takes a balanced view of life—serious without being stuffy, warmhearted without being overly sentimental.

So go ahead. Try a new hair-do or splurge on a stylish dress. Have fun and look your best. But never forget that true style is a reflection of your relationship with God. Brains, beauty, and spiritual balance have it all over the latest trend and the hottest look.

I Will

Remember that while I can be distracted by appearances, God sees the heart. _____ yes _____ no

Live life from the heart instead of trying to impress or manipulate others. _____ yes _____ no

Cultivate my spirit by spending time alone with God. _____ yes _____ no

Appreciate beauty and creativity wherever I find them. _____ yes _____ no

Remember that kindness and compassion are great beautifiers. _____ yes _____ no

Enjoy my femininity without taking myself too seriously. _____ yes _____ no

Be aware of others who may be struggling even if they look like they have it all together. _____ yes _____ no

Things to Do

☐ Read the Bible story of Esther to learn about the power of a beautiful woman who was willing to sacrifice her life to save her people.

☐ Speak a kind word the next time you are tempted to gossip about someone.

☐ Take an exercise class.

☐ Cultivate your mind by reading a good book.

☐ Become an adult sponsor for youth activities so you can mentor younger women.

☐ Go shopping for clothes that are flattering, comfortable, and expressive of your style.

☐ Leave an extra tip for the hairdresser the next time you get your hair cut.

Things to Remember

Do not let your adornment be merely outward—arranging the hair, wearing gold, or putting on fine apparel—rather let it be the hidden person of the heart, with the incorruptible beauty of a gentle and quiet spirit, which is very precious in the sight of God.

1 PETER 3:3–4 NKJV

Charm can be deceiving, and beauty fades away, but a woman who honors the LORD deserves to be praised.

PROVERBS 31:30 CEV

Every wise woman builds her house, but the foolish pulls it down with her hands.

PROVERBS 14:1 NKJV

Though some tongues just love the taste of gossip, Christians have better use for language than that. Don't talk dirty or silly. That kind of talk doesn't fit our style. Thanksgiving is our dialect.

EPHESIANS 5:4 THE MESSAGE

Happy are those who do not follow the advice of the wicked, or take the path that sinners tread, or sit in the seat of scoffers; but their delight is in the law of the LORD, and on his law they meditate day and night.

PSALM 1:1–2 NRSV

Taking joy in life is a woman's best cosmetic.

—ROSALIND RUSSELL

Goodness in the heart works its way up into the face and prints it own beauty there.

—ANONYMOUS

Valuing Life

Open Your Eyes, Open Your Heart

Oh, that men would give thanks to the LORD for His goodness, and for His wonderful works to the children of men!

—PSALM 107:8 NKJV

There is so much beauty and wonder in the world around you. Beauty reminds you that God loves you, giving you a tiny taste of what one day eternity with Christ will be like. Yet you often forget to see and value the bounties God has spread before you. You get caught up in the concerns of daily life, aware only that the next work deadline looms in front of you, the children need new shoes, the car needs repair, and the bills are due at the end of the month.

There are so many wonders in this world. Are you awake? Are your eyes open? Is your heart receptive? "Beauty is all about us, but how many are blind to it!" exclaimed cellist Pablo Casals. God saw what he had made and saw that it was good. Do you take the time to see what God has created? Are you able to be receptive and totally present in the moment? All kinds of wonderful and amazing things are going on around you. An important part of the spiritual life is learning to pay attention. "Consider the lilies," Jesus said. Take a moment to stop and stare in awe and behold the works of the Lord.

Even when your lives are stressful and your problems seem overwhelming, you need to remember that pleasure lies in the heart. Your attitude affects your perception. Luci Swindoll said, "To experience happiness we must train ourselves to live in this moment, not running ahead in anticipation some future date nor lagging behind in the paralysis of the past. With wholeness and sensitivity we must live in the here and now."

The mundane things of life—a sack of groceries, a phone call, a carpool, a meeting—can be reminders of God's generous blessings. That van full of children you are ferrying to the soccer game is full of bright faces and eager young hearts. A friend on the other end of a phone reminds you that you are rich in support and loyalty. A crowded grocery aisle can be seen as a place of plenty and choice. These small wonders can make you smile with joy, if you open your eyes to the value of life in the here and now. Look into your heart and see that you, too, are a wonder created and loved by God.

Today is a good day to value life, just as it presents itself to you. Open your eyes. Open your heart. Receive God's priceless gift of life.

I Will

Pay attention to my life.   *yes* _____   *no* _____

Be receptive and totally present in the moment.   *yes* _____   *no* _____

See God in the details.   *yes* _____   *no* _____

Be curious about life and all its mysteries.   *yes* _____   *no* _____

Open my heart to God's grace as revealed
in His creation.   *yes* _____   *no* _____

Be aware of small moments of grace and little
epiphanies around me.   *yes* _____   *no* _____

Be aware of what is going on within me.   *yes* _____   *no* _____

Things to Do

☐ Mark out some time in your daily calendar for "life-appreciation breaks."

☐ Go for a long walk in a park or forest.

☐ Buy a single rose to remind you of the beauty of God's creation.

☐ Read Psalm 148.

☐ Read a book on natural history.

☐ Spend time apart with a loved one, savoring with an appreciative heart who and what he or she is.

☐ Treat yourself to a new flavor of ice cream or try an ethnic cuisine that you haven't enjoyed before.

Things to Remember

God saw everything that He had made, and indeed it was very good.

GENESIS 1:31 NKJV

I will praise You, for I am fearfully and wonderfully made; marvelous are Your works, and that my soul knows very well.

PSALM 139:14 NKJV

Jesus said, "Consider the lilies, how they grow: they neither toil nor spin; and yet I say to you, even Solomon in all his glory was not arrayed like one of these."

LUKE 12:27 NKJV

Jesus said, "First things first. Your business is life, not death. Follow me. Pursue life."

MATTHEW 8:22 THE MESSAGE

The song was raised, with trumpets and cymbals and other musical instruments, in praise to the Lord. "For he is good, for his steadfast love endures forever."

2 CHRONICLES 5:13 NRSV

Happy is the man who is always reverent, but he who hardens his heart will fall into calamity.

PROVERBS 28:14 NKJV

To believe in God means to take sides with life and to end our alliance with death. It means to stop killing and wanting to kill, and to do battle with apathy which is so akin to killing.

—DOROTHEE SOELLE

At the back of our brains, so to speak, there is a forgotten blaze or burst of astonishment at our own existence. The object of the artistic and the spiritual life is to dig for this submerged sunrise of wonder.

—G. K. CHESTERTON

Meditation

Think on These Things

"In your anger do not sin!" Do not let the sun go down while you are still angry.

—*Ephesians 4:26* NIV

Meditation is a quietly powerful way to deepen your spiritual life and draw closer to God. From the psalmist who meditated on God's law and character, to Mary, the mother of Jesus, who pondered all things in her heart, the Bible teaches the value of time spent in meditation. There are many ways to approach meditation. You can memorize passages of Scripture. You can begin or end your day with reading a devotional or writing in your journal. When you set aside time for meditation, you open your heart and your mind to the Spirit's influence.

You can meditate on Scripture. But your spiritual reading can also include great books and writers of all kinds. Spiritual reading is less about the content of what you read and more about the attitude of your heart when you read. Meditating on what you read transforms reading into an activity of love and attention. Along with the Bible, look for classics that have stood the test of time. Authors of spiritual classics from history include John Bunyan,

Brother Lawrence, John Calvin, Martin Luther, Charles Finney, John Milton, and Blaise Pascal. More modern authors include C. S. Lewis, Billy Graham, Oswald Chambers, Dietrich Bonhoffer, Mother Teresa, Dorothy Sayers, G. K. Chesterton, and Flannery O'Connor. As you read, think about what insights God might want to offer to you through the printed page and how these things might apply to your daily life.

There are many other ways to meditate. Some women keep a daily journal, writing about their activities, letting their thoughts flow out onto the page. Other women prefer a more active way to meditate, taking long walks in nature and mulling over their lives. Perhaps you would enjoy bringing a pocket New Testament and Psalms on a walk and meditating on a Scripture passage as you look out on the wonderful view. Go into a quiet church to pray and meditate. Memorize promises from Scripture and think about them as you do household tasks. Meditation can be as simple as making a cup of tea, lighting a candle, and sitting in a comfortable chair for a time of Bible reading.

"When you meditate, imagine that Jesus Christ in person is about to talk to you about the most important thing in the world," said François Fènelon. "Give him your complete attention." Know that God wants to speak personally to you in every moment of the day. A regular time of meditation is a way of welcoming His presence into your life.

I Will

Be open to new insight from unexpected sources
when I seek out spiritual reading.

yes   *no*

Allow God to speak to my heart by meditating on
His Word.

yes   *no*

Be still and listen to God.

yes   *no*

Contemplate the meaning in the daily events of
my life.

yes   *no*

Have a teachable heart and a childlike attitude.

yes   *no*

Leave behind expectations and come to my time of
meditation with an open mind.

yes   *no*

Nurture intimacy with God.

yes   *no*

Things to Do

☐ Set aside a regular time for daily meditation.

☐ Take your Bible or a spiritual book with you to read on a walk in the woods.

☐ Buy a blank notebook and begin a meditation journal.

☐ Create a simple home altar for worship and meditation.

☐ Seek out a spiritual classic, such as Brother Lawrence's The Practice of the Presence of God or Oswald Chambers's My Utmost for His Highest, to complement your Bible reading.

☐ Listen to Scripture CDs in the car on your way to work.

☐ Take a short break this afternoon for a minute of meditation and mental refreshment.

Things to Remember

This book of the law shall not depart out of your mouth; you shall meditate on it day and night, so that you may be careful to act in accordance with all that is written in it. For then you shall make your way prosperous, and then you shall be successful.

JOSHUA 1:8 NRSV

Mary kept all these things and pondered them in her heart.

LUKE 2:19 NKJV

He has made His wonderful works to be remembered; the LORD is gracious and full of compassion.

PSALM 111:4 NKJV

We know only a portion of the truth, and what we say about God is always incomplete.

1 CORINTHIANS 13:9 THE MESSAGE

Knowing isn't everything. If it becomes everything, some people end up as know-it-alls who treat others as know-nothings. Real knowledge isn't that insensitive.

1 CORINTHIANS 8:7 THE MESSAGE

Meditate within your heart on your bed and be still.

PSALM 4:4 NKJV

Spiritual reading does not mean reading on spiritual or religious subjects, but reading any book that comes to hand in a spiritual way, which is to say, listening to the Spirit, alert to intimations of God.

—EUGENE PETERSON

In the rush and noise of life, as you have intervals, step home within yourselves and be still. Wait upon God, and feel his good presence; this will carry you evenly through your day's business.

—WILLIAM PENN

Sadness

Every Tear Is Treasured

You number my wanderings; put my tears into your bottle; are they not in Your book?

—*Psalm 56:8* NKJV

A heavy heart is a load greater than you can carry alone. When your days are dark with disappointment, God understands your sorrow. He does not read you a lecture or tell you to be more cheerful. He has carried your grief and borne your sorrow. He knows your weakness and helps you.

Life has its troubles and trials. No one is immune from suffering. Sadness is a part of life. God doesn't say you won't have sorrow, but He does say that He will be with you in your sorrow and comfort you in your grief.

Perhaps you are struggling with a disappointment. A relationship has been broken and you rehearse the things you regret over and over in your mind. Or you lost your job and you have to reinvent your life while you try to pay the bills. Perhaps illness has curtailed your ability to do the things you love. You may be sad from the loss of a loved one. If you are a mother who has lost her child, there is no grief quite so deep and dark. You may be widowed or divorced, coping with loneliness and an empty heart. Though you pretend to feel positive, all you really want to do is have a good cry. God is with you in all your sorrows.

Learn to comfort yourself and allow God to comfort you. Here are some simple ways to cope during times of stress and sadness.

Take care of your health. Get some physical exercise and eat as well as you can. Make sure you get plenty of rest if at all possible.

Take a break away from the problem or trouble. Sometimes it is possible to get so focused on sadness that you can forget to look at the larger picture. Read a good book. Take a walk or go see a movie. Buy fresh flowers. Pet a puppy or hold a baby. Getting fresh perspective helps you cope with sadness.

Ask for help. In times of sadness, it's too easy to isolate yourself just when you need people the most. Have tea with a friend. Go to church and worship with others. Meet with your pastor, chaplain, or counselor. Hugs and affection support your body as well as your emotions.

Nurture your spirit through meditation, Bible reading, and prayer.

Know that God is with you in your times of sadness. He promises to never leave you or forsake you. He treasures all of your tears.

I Will

Remember that God is with me in my sadness.   yes   no

Trust that God will comfort me in times of sorrow.   yes   no

Believe the promises of God.   yes   no

Understand that tears are one way God helps me heal.   yes   no

Commit myself to taking care of my health even when I feel too sad to care.   yes   no

Rest in God's care.   yes   no

Look for the small blessings that surround me even when I am sad.   yes   no

Things to Do

☐ *Make an appointment to get together with an understanding friend for a time of prayer, comfort, and encouragement.*

☐ *List twenty things you are thankful for today.*

☐ *Memorize Romans 8:28.*

☐ *Take a nap the next time you are feeling overwhelmed.*

☐ *Make a pot of homemade soup to soothe your soul and nourish your body.*

☐ *Make an appointment to speak to a pastor or counselor.*

☐ *Reread a favorite novel that comforts your heart.*

Things to Remember

Praise be to the God and Father of our Lord Jesus Christ, the Father of compassion and the God of all comfort, who comforts us in all our troubles, so that we can comfort those in any trouble with the comfort we ourselves have received from God.

2 CORINTHIANS 1:3–4 NIV

I will be glad and rejoice in Your mercy, for You have considered my trouble; You have known my soul in adversities.

PSALM 31:7 NKJV

Let us therefore come boldly to the throne of grace, that we may obtain mercy and find grace to help in time of need.

HEBREWS 4:16 NKJV

This is my comfort in my affliction, for Your word has given me life.

PSALM 119:50 NKJV

He shall call upon Me, and I will answer him; I will be with him in trouble; I will deliver him and honor him.

PSALM 91:15 NKJV

My flesh and my heart faileth; but God is the strength of my heart, and my portion for ever.

PSALM 73:26 KJV

Heaven knows we need never be ashamed of our tears, for they are rain upon the blinding dust of earth, overlying our hard hearts.

—CHARLES DICKENS

The tearful praying Christian, whose distress prevents his words, will be clearly understood by the Most High.

—C. H. SPURGEON

Hopes and Dreams

If You Could Have Three Wishes

~~~~~~

Delight yourself also in the LORD, and He shall give you the desires of your heart.

—*PSALM 37:4* NKJV

In many fairy and folk tales, the heroine is offered the opportunity to wish for her heart's desire. What would you do with three wishes? What would you wish for? The psalmist tells you that if you delight in the Lord, He will grant you the desires of your heart. What hopes, dreams, and wishes do you wish God would grant to you?

God isn't a genie in a bottle, carelessly granting wishes with no concern for the well-being and character of the person making the wish. God wants you to partner with Him to make your dreams come true. He gives you the desire and you grow into the dream, because He has plans for you that are more wonderful and delightful than those you could imagine on your own. You might wish to be more beautiful, to have a bigger home, or to enjoy greater prosperity. But God may desire that you have more beautiful aspirations, a more generous heart, and greater awareness of the blessings you have already received.

The childlike heart loves dreams and fantasies and stories of wishes instantly granted. As you grow older, you learn that work and perseverance and trust are the ways most dreams become reality. If you have a desire in your heart, a dream that you wish would become reality, here are some ways you can partner with God to make the dream come true.

First, know what you want. Articulate it and clarify it. Visualize the end result. Set specific goals to turn your dream into a reality.

Next, take the dream to God and let Him show you whether it is worthy. Continue to come to Him in prayer as you work toward the goals you have set. Any worthwhile dream grows you as you grow it. Like a seed planted in rich soil, plant your dreams in the soil of God's love and guidance.

Do the work. Realize that it may take longer than you had planned. Remember that every detour and delay is an opportunity to learn something—often a lesson that is necessary for making your dream come true. Persevere. Don't give up.

Finally, trust God to bring the dream to fruition in just the right time, just the right way. Delight in His ways and He will give you the desires of your heart. You can always trust God with your hopes, your wishes, and your dreams. Life may disappoint you, but God will never let you down.

I Will

Dare to dream big dreams because I have a big God.   _yes_   _no_

Be willing to work hard.   _yes_   _no_

Have patience with delays and problems.   _yes_   _no_

Commit myself wholeheartedly to achieving a goal
that is dear to my heart.   _yes_   _no_

Trust God to guide me.   _yes_   _no_

Trust in God's perfect timing in my life.   _yes_   _no_

Be thankful for the blessings and help I receive.   _yes_   _no_

Things to Do

☐ Answer this question in your journal: If you had three wishes, what would you wish for?

☐ Write down a cherished goal and break it into steps to accomplish it.

☐ Take the goal and the steps you wrote down and pray about what God would have you do.

☐ Do the first item on your list of steps to accomplish your goal.

☐ Make a collage that represents your goals and dreams.

☐ Take a class that will give you a new skill to help you reach your goal.

☐ Call some friends and set up a time to get together for mutual encouragement.

Things to Remember

It shall come to pass that before they call, I will answer; and while they are still speaking, I will hear.

ISAIAH 65:24 NKJV

This hope we have as an anchor of the soul, both sure and steadfast, and which enters the Presence behind the veil.

HEBREWS 6:19 NKJV

We know that if our earthly house, this tent, is destroyed, we have a building from God, a house not made with hands, eternal in the heavens.

2 CORINTHIANS 5:1 NKJV

Therefore do not cast away your confidence, which has great reward. For you have need of endurance, so that after you have done the will of God, you may receive the promise.

HEBREWS 10:35–36 NKJV

The desire accomplished is sweet to the soul.

PROVERBS 13:19 KJV

Let us hold fast the confession of our hope without wavering, for He who promised is faithful.

HEBREWS 10:23 NKJV

Man finds it hard to get what he wants, because he does not want the best; God finds it hard to give, because He would give the best, and man will not take it.

—GEORGE MACDONALD

What can be hoped for which is not believed?

—SAINT AUGUSTINE

Treasures in the Darkness

I will give you the treasures of darkness and hidden riches of secret places, that you may know that I, the LORD, who call you by your name, am the God of Israel.

—*ISAIAH 45:3* NKJV

Troubles come in all shapes and sizes. Trouble can be as small as a run in your stocking or as big as an emergency trip to the hospital. The same flat tire that made you a few minutes late for the grand opening sale at the department store could also be the few minutes that kept you from harm on the highway. When troubles come, you have a choice—to let troubles destroy you or transform you. A diamond is just a piece of coal that has undergone pressure. When you are handed a lump of coal in the form of trouble, it's an opportunity to see how God can transform it into spiritual treasure. Ugly things can become jewels reflecting the light of God, if you are willing to go into the darkness with Him and find the hidden treasure.

First, acknowledge that the trouble is real and needs to be faced. You can't ask God for help if you keep denying you have a problem. Admit that you are hurt or disappointed or angry. God can take it. He is not afraid of your honest questions, and He doesn't expect you to gloss over the problem in the name of being spiritual. Read the book of Psalms and you'll see that anger and sorrow are expressed as well as praise and thankfulness. If you can be real with God, then He can really help you.

Next, assess the situation. Ask God for wisdom and guidance. Take responsibility for what you can do in the situation. Do you need to admit a fault or ask someone for forgiveness? Do you need to make a wrong right? Is there a positive action you can take to ease the situation, relieve the trouble, or make things better? Avoid complaining. Instead, do what is in your power to do.

Perhaps there is nothing you can do right now to make things better. You may need to wait for the right timing. Or maybe something else must happen first or someone else needs to do his or her part. Sometimes a broken thing is broken and can't be fixed. Acknowledge what is out of your hands and put it into God's hands.

In the darkness, out of sight, God will use the pressures and problems to create the lovely jewel of a quiet spirit, a strengthened character, and a wiser heart. One day you will see—whether in this life or in the shining, glorious crown of glory you will behold in the next life. There are treasures to be discovered in the darkness, and troubles can be transformed into glorious victories if you can walk through them trusting God.

I Will

Trust God with my troubles.   yes   no

Be positive when I'm tempted to complain.   yes   no

Be willing to take extra effort with my appearance
when I'm feeling downhearted.   yes   no

Look for the lessons my troubles can teach me. yes   no

Be compassionate with others who are sad, frustrated,
or troubled.   yes   no

Remember that troubles are temporary and that my
true hope rests in eternal things.   yes   no

Be grateful for the small things that I normally take
for granted.   yes   no

Things to Do

☐ The next time you are tempted to complain, quickly list five things you
are grateful for.

☐ Read Psalm 42.

☐ Do one kind deed without being discovered.

☐ Write in your journal about three things that trouble you and how you
feel about them.

☐ Find and memorize a Bible verse to answer each of those three troubles
with a promise from God.

☐ Have a quiet half hour by yourself and relax.

☐ Dress as becomingly as possible today—you'll feel better and make
others feel better too.

Things to Remember

Cast your burden upon the LORD, and He shall sustain you; He shall never permit the righteous to be moved.

PSALM 55:22 NKJV

Do not become sluggish, but imitate those who through faith and patience inherit the promises.

HEBREWS 6:12 NKJV

Without faith it is impossible to please Him, for he who comes to God must believe that He is, and that He is a rewarder of those who diligently seek Him.

HEBREWS 11:6 NKJV

The people that walked in darkness have seen a great light; they that dwell in the land of the shadow of death, upon them hath the light shined.

ISAIAH 9:2 KJV

Everything exposed by light becomes visible, for it is light that makes everything visible.

EPHESIANS 5:13 NIV

We do not lose heart. Even though our outward man is perishing, yet the inward man is being renewed day by day.

2 CORINTHIANS 4:16 NKJV

In times of trouble, remember that God is too kind to be cruel, too wise to make a mistake, and too deep to explain himself.

—AUTHOR UNKNOWN

I would rather walk with God in the dark than go alone in the light.

—MARY GARDINER BRAINARD

Identity

A Very Special Person

You are a chosen generation, a royal priesthood, a holy nation, His own special people, that you may proclaim the praises of Him who called you out of darkness into His marvelous light.

—*1 PETER 2:9* NKJV

This culture likes to label and define people. Advertisers and marketers talk about demographics, separating people into categories according to age, interests, and buying patterns. You were graded and evaluated when you were in school, and as an adult your job description sorts you into department, function, and salary level. If asked to tell someone who you are, you could describe yourself many ways. "I am the leader of a woman's group." "I am a wife and mother." "I am an executive board member." You could describe yourself in terms of race, religion, physical appearance, career achievements, or intelligence. But the real question is not "How do I or others define my identity?" Instead, the real question is "How does God define my identity?"

The Bible says that your identity is in Christ, not in the circumstances of your birth, your economic standing in the world, or your ability to please others. This positive identity transcends all human categories, freeing you to live out your true calling from God. Your identity in Christ is a constant source of strength. Your hope is not in your power or righteousness or self-discipline, but in God's power working in and through you.

As a woman you may dwell on what you are not: not pretty enough, not spiritual enough, not thin enough, not a good enough wife or mother. But God sees you differently. He sees you as uniquely created and beautiful in His eyes. You are made in the image of God. You are forgiven and called in Christ.

When you claim your identity in Christ, you can have a peaceful confidence in His declaration of who you are. Circumstances may change and you may make mistakes, but God sees you as perfect and complete in His Son. This identity offers a solid foundation that gives you room to grow and change, encouraging new interests and adventures. It's large enough for a lifetime and allows you to explore who you are and who you want to become.

Your identity as God's beloved child will improve your relationships, freeing you from the need to manipulate others. You no longer have to conform to stereotypes of who and what you should be. You can revel in your own individuality and accept others' differences. You can stand for what you believe without the need to prove yourself superior to others.

Enjoy the freedom and explore the potential of your God-given identity, knowing that you are a very special person in the eyes of God.

I Will

Be confident because I know that God has called me.   yes   no

Enjoy my individuality.   yes   no

Invest in cultivating my gifts and talents.   yes   no

Do my best and trust God with the results.   yes   no

Relax in God's love instead of trying too hard.   yes   no

Be empathetic to the struggles of others.   yes   no

Enjoy my freedom in Christ.   yes   no

Know that God thinks I am special.   yes   no

Things to Do

☐   Tell someone why you are special today.

☐   Ask someone why he or she is special.

☐   Ask yourself why you are here on earth and write your answer in your journal.

☐   Write a thank-you note to someone who has encouraged you.

☐   Ask yourself what qualities of Christ are evident in your life.

☐   List ten of your strengths.

☐   Make a plan to maximize one of your strengths.

Things to Remember

It is better to trust in the Lord than to put confidence in man.

PSALM 118:8 NKJV

Jesus said, "You did not choose Me, but I chose you and appointed you that you should go and bear fruit, and that your fruit should remain, that whatever you ask the Father in My name He may give you."

JOHN 15:16 NKJV

Now we see in a mirror, dimly, but then face to face. Now I know in part, but then I shall know just as I am known.

1 CORINTHIANS 13:12 NKJV

What you say about yourself means nothing in God's work. It's what God says about you that makes the difference.

2 CORINTHIANS 5:17 THE MESSAGE

It's in Christ that we find out who we are and what we are living for. Long before we first heard of Christ and got our hopes up, he had his eye on us, had designs on us for glorious living, part of the overall purpose he is working out in everything and everyone.

EPHESIANS 1:11 THE MESSAGE

To work in the world lovingly means that we are defining what we will be for, rather than reacting to what we are against.

—CHRISTINA BALDWIN

Christians have an entirely new basis for identity. This basis is a foundational reality which transcends any culture's evaluation of a person.

—BARBARA COOK

Treasures from God

Agree with each other. Love each other. Be deep spirited friends.
—PHILIPPIANS 2:2 THE MESSAGE

Friendship is a gift from God. Friends laugh with you, cry with you, stand beside you. A good friend will confront you when you need to be told a difficult truth. Good friends help you grow and believe the best in you. They are treasures who enrich your life immeasurably.

Treasure your friendships. Make time to go out for lunch or tea with your female friends. It doesn't matter how old a woman is, she still needs to giggle like a teenager with trusted girlfriends. You need someone you can let your hair down with.

Make room for many kinds of friends. Longtime friends know you like nobody else. New friends help you explore new facets of who you are. Friends who share certain seasons of life often end up bonding for life. Mothers meet other mothers and share child-raising questions. Friends who share hobbies or careers help each other develop their skills and contacts. Dinner with other couples, picnics with church friends, and community get-togethers offer a kaleidoscope of friendship that enlivens you and makes life worthwhile even in the toughest times.

Friendship is a two-way street. If you want to have friends, you need to be a friend.

Be willing to reach out to other people. You never know when you'll discover a new friend.

Be loyal to your friends. Don't judge, but choose to believe the best.

Invest time in your friendships. Remember that relationships need nurturing if they are to stay healthy.

Be flexible. Allow friends room to grow and change.

Cheer each other on. Encourage one another. Be enthusiastic and supportive instead of negative and doubting.

Remember that small thoughtful acts of kindness are more important than grand gestures. Friendship is built on equality and caring for one another.

Allow friendship to have its seasons. Sometimes a friend needs more space. Sometimes your friend needs more time and attention. And sometimes you have to be willing to allow a friendship to end. Trust that as some friends leave your life, new friends will enter.

Always be honest and open with your friends. Little white lies and whispering behind someone's back will poison even the best of friendships.

Cultivate your own character so that you will be the kind of person who attracts and keeps good friends. Seek out friends who bring out the best in you. Choose and create friendships that honor God and make your world a better place.

I Will

Be thankful to God for my friends. _____ yes _____ no

Be alert to the needs of my friends. _____ yes _____ no

Lighten up, laugh, and let down my hair with
trusted girlfriends. _____ yes _____ no

Make friendship a high priority in my life. _____ yes _____ no

Be honest with my friends. _____ yes _____ no

Believe for the best and encourage the best in my
friendships. _____ yes _____ no

Appreciate the unique qualities of each of my
friends. _____ yes _____ no

Things to Do

☐ Think about what makes a good friendship and write about that in
your journal.

☐ Call your best girlfriends and make a date to go out to lunch or tea
together.

☐ Make an appointment to spend some time with a friend you haven't
seen in a while.

☐ Buy a thoughtful little gift to give a friend.

☐ Send an encouraging note to someone who needs it.

☐ Put a framed picture of you with friends on your desk at work or in a
prominent place at home to remind you of good times and good friends.

Things to Remember

A friend loves at all times, and a brother is born for adversity.

PROVERBS 17:17 NKJV

Everyone helped his neighbor, and said to his brother, "Be of good courage!"

ISAIAH 41:6 NKJV

Let all that you do be done with love.

1 CORINTHIANS 16:14 NKJV

Just as lotions and fragrance give sensual delight, a sweet friendship refreshes the soul.

PROVERBS 27:9 THE MESSAGE

Through love, serve one another.

GALATIANS 5:13 NKJV

Friends come and friends go, but a true friend sticks by you like family.

PROVERBS 18:24 THE MESSAGE

Like good stewards of the manifold grace of God, serve one another with whatever gift each of you has received.

1 PETER 4:10 NRSV

Abraham believed God, and it was imputed unto him for righteousness: and he was called the Friend of God.

JAMES 2:23 KJV

The impulse of love that leads us to the doorway of a friend is the voice of God within and we need not be afraid to follow it.

—AGNES SANFORD

The only way to have a friend is to be a friend.

—RALPH WALDO EMERSON

Enjoying God

Praise the LORD! Praise the name of the LORD; praise Him, O you servants of the LORD!

—*PSALM 135:1* NKJV

What an exuberant, joyful command! Praise the Lord! God is worthy to be praised. Not only for what He does, but for who He is. Your praise is a response to the character of God, who He is and what He has done in your life to touch you and to heal you.

We tend to look for God in the phenomenal and grandiose. So when it comes to praising God, we often think of Cecil B. DeMille extravaganzas complete with "Lights! Camera! Action!" We think of an end-times book of the Revelation experience with a cast of thousands in full costume, blasting trumpets, and flying flags. Though you are promised in the book of Revelation that you will one day experience a greater scene of praise than any moviemaker can imagine, you can also praise God in the ordinary and common things of life, here and now.

Everyday praise includes singing songs to God as you do dishes or vacuum the floor. You can praise God when you put on your makeup—look in the mirror and thank

Him for the face you were born with, the face you are putting on for the world, and the face that reflects a loving heart no matter what your outward style may be. You can praise Him every day with a grace before meals. Offer thanksgiving for the small blessings you enjoy—from the cup of coffee you drink to the sheets and blankets that keep you warm at night. Did your car start this morning? Praise God. Did your car need to be towed to a mechanic for repair instead? Praise God anyway, especially if you have an honest mechanic who will fix your car for a fair price. Praise God on the freeway or in the school parking lot. Praise God in the grocery store or at the churchwomen's committee meeting. Praise Him for the child's sticky kiss or the husband's morning hug or the phone call from a friend. In everything give thanks. Praise the Lord!

The whole Bible is punctuated with outbursts of praise. It comes spontaneously from the joy that characterizes God's people. Does the joy of the Lord characterize you? Do you take pleasure and delight in God's creation—and remember to share that pleasure with God? When you praise Him, you participate in the coming of God's kingdom to earth, even if only in a small acknowledgment that He is your Lord and worthy of your praise.

I Will

Praise God with all my heart. _yes_ _no_

Be alert to small blessings in my day. _yes_ _no_

Have a thankful heart. _yes_ _no_

Avoid complaining. _yes_ _no_

*Be aware of opportunities to praise God in
the midst of my day.* _yes_ _no_

Joyfully sing songs of praise to God. _yes_ _no_

Take delight in being God's child. _yes_ _no_

Things to Do

☐ *Write your own personal prayer of praise and say it to God.*

☐ *Memorize a psalm of praise (perhaps Psalm 117).*

☐ *Number a page from 1 to 100. Write down 100 things you praise God
for in your life.*

☐ *Join with other believers in praise and worship this Sunday.*

☐ *Write a letter to someone you admire, in appreciation for his or her
contribution to your life.*

☐ *Sing a song of praise to God the next time you do the dishes or other
household chore alone.*

☐ *Do a topical Bible study on praise.*

Things to Remember

Holy, holy, holy, Lord God Almighty,
who was and is and is to come!

REVELATION 4:8 NKJV

We all, with unveiled face, beholding as
in a mirror the glory of the Lord, are
being transformed into the same image
from glory to glory, just as by the Spirit
of the Lord.

2 CORINTHIANS 3:18 NKJV

Mary said, "My soul magnifies the Lord,
and my spirit has rejoiced in God my
Savior."

LUKE 1:46–47 NKJV

Let us continually offer the sacrifice of
praise to God, that is, the fruit of our
lips, giving thanks to His name.

HEBREWS 13:15 NKJV

Be glad and rejoice forever in what I
create; for behold, I create Jerusalem as a
rejoicing, and her people a joy.

ISAIAH 65:18 NKJV

I will praise the name of God with a
song, and will magnify Him with
thanksgiving.

PSALM 69:30 NKJV

Praise not merely expresses but completes the enjoyment; it is its appointed consummation. . . . In commending us to glorify Him, God is inviting us to enjoy Him.

—C. S. LEWIS

You don't learn to praise in a day, especially since you may have been complaining for years! New habits take time to develop. But you can begin today, and practice tomorrow, and the next day, until it becomes a part of you.

—ERWIN W. LUTZER

Encouragement

A Warm Shoulder in a Cold World

Let us consider one another in order to stir up love and good works, not forsaking the assembling of ourselves together, as is the manner of some, but exhorting one another, and so much the more as you see the Day approaching.

—HEBREWS 10:24–25 NKJV

Encouragement is a gift that we can offer others and ourselves. A listening ear, a warm shoulder to lean on, a helping hand, and an understanding heart offer support through the challenges and changes of life. When you make a conscious choice to be an encourager, you become God's helping hand of support, inspiring courage, hope, and confidence in the midst of a weary world.

When your best girlfriend tells you about her pet project, you respond with an enthusiastic, "What a great idea! I know you'll make it happen." When the man in your life shares his hopes and dreams, you reinforce his self-worth and repel negative thoughts. You quietly say, "Yes, you can" instead of "Yes, but." You're not afraid to say something positive to others. These phrases are often a part of your conversation: "I love you because . . ." "I see in you . . ." "You're so good at . . ." "I like the way you . . ." "I know you will . . ."

Here are some tips for being a better encourager:

• Be specific and tell people in detail exactly what you like about them, what you have observed that can help them.

• Be honest and kind. No flattery allowed. You want to point out the positives, yet be someone who offers a dependable perspective, not a flattering lie.

• Be positive and confident. Express doubts with care and try to offer alternatives when you think someone is being unrealistic.

• Be spontaneous. Listen to what your heart says and be willing to speak it.

• Don't worry about how your encouragement is received. People are insecure and often don't know how to take praise. They often need time to revise the way they look at themselves. Just keep believing the best for them, even when they are afraid to believe it for themselves.

• Be consistent. Focus on the positive; make it a lifestyle. Make encouragement a habit.

• Offer suggestions, not advice. Honor each person's choices and believe in others' ability to navigate their own course. You may disagree with their decisions, but you have to respect their choices.

• Finally, be your own best encourager. Count your blessings. Be careful of the company you keep—don't spend too much time with negative people who tear one another down. Focus on the larger vision, knowing that God has called you to a unique work in this world. Give yourself time, space, and grace. Release your discouragement to God. Ask Him to help you find purpose in your pain and disappointments. Believe for the best.

I Will

Cultivate the art of encouraging others.   _yes_   _no_

Be honest, yet kind and helpful.   _yes_   _no_

Release my discouragement to God.   _yes_   _no_

Focus on the positive.   _yes_   _no_

Make encouragement a habit.   _yes_   _no_

Believe the best of others.   _yes_   _no_

Be willing to speak up and encourage others.   _yes_   _no_

Count my blessings.   _yes_   _no_

Things to Do

☐ Do a word study on encouragement.

☐ Call a friend and encourage her.

☐ Form an encouragers circle to meet on a regular basis.

☐ Offer to pray for someone else's needs.

☐ List specific ways someone is a blessing to you. Share the list with that person.

☐ Write a note of encouragement to five people.

☐ Give five people a loving hug today.

Things to Remember

Therefore let us pursue the things which make for peace and the things by which one may edify another.

ROMANS 14:9 NKJV

He answered, "Do not fear, for those who are with us are more than those who are with them."

2 KINGS 6:16 NKJV

They encouraged the followers and begged them to remain faithful.

ACTS 14:22 CEV

We treated each of you as a father treats his own children. We pleaded with you, encouraged you, and urged you to live your lives in a way that God would consider worthy.

1 THESSALONIANS 2:11–12 NLT

Let's see how inventive we can be in encouraging love and helping out.

HEBREWS 10:24 THE MESSAGE

Proclaim the message; be persistent whether the time is favorable or unfavorable; convince, rebuke, and encourage, with the utmost patience in teaching.

2 TIMOTHY 4:2 NRSV

Encouragement is oxygen to the soul.

—GEORGE M. ADAMS

Everybody can be great. Because anybody can serve. . . . You only need a heart full of grace. A soul generated by love.

—MARTIN LUTHER KING

Patience

Waiting on God

Hope deferred makes the heart sick, but when the desire comes, it is a tree of life.

—*Proverbs 13:12* NKJV

How many times have you found yourself asking impatiently, "How long is this going to take?" Yet God's timing is different from yours, and you may often find yourself in need of patience. You may think that you are too busy to wait, to allow things to grow naturally. You force solutions, often creating more problems than you solve. But God works in His own time and in His own way. He teaches you the value of patience. In the larger perspective of life, eternal lessons teach you that patience is required for the things that are really important.

It takes time to raise a child, nurture a relationship, grow a career, and create a community. The Scriptures use the image of a farmer patiently waiting for seed, soil, sun, and rain to do its work. The field must be plowed, the seed sown, the land fertilized and watered, the soil weeded, and the crop tended before it comes to full fruition. So it is with you.

When you cultivate patience, you are growing the fruit

of the Spirit in your life. Patience is not passiveness, but a proactive faith that is willing to trust God in the midst of difficulties and delays.

How do you cultivate patience during times of waiting? Here are some ideas:

• Take it one day at a time. Instead of trying to second-guess the future, look at what you have right now. What can be accomplished today? Concentrate only on what you are able to do today and put tomorrow in God's hands.

• Do what you can and let go of trying to control the outcome. All you can do is do your best and leave the rest up to God. In most of the important things in life, we are dependent on God's grace.

• Write in your journal. Write about your feelings of impatience. Imagine the fulfillment of your desires and write that down. Remember times when your patience was rewarded. A journal is a safe place to vent, to dream, and to track answers to prayer requests.

• Meditate on Scripture. The Bible offers a timeless way of looking at life, and we absorb that larger perspective when we feed our spirits with the Word.

• Pray. Bring your worries, frustrations, and anxiety to God. Tell Him how you honestly feel and ask His help in being patient. Speak words of faith affirming that you trust Him to bring things to full fruition in His perfect timing.

I Will

Cultivate a patient attitude.   yes   no

Trust God with my future.   yes   no

Bring my worries and anxieties to God in prayer.   yes   no

Take life one day at a time.   yes   no

Avoid second-guessing the future.   yes   no

Affirm my trust in God with words of faith.   yes   no

Depend on God's grace and divine timing.   yes   no

Do my best and leave the rest up to God.   yes   no

Things to Do

☐ Write in your journal about a time when God rewarded your patient work and waiting.

☐ Write in your journal about a time when you tried to make something happen and it fell apart.

☐ Meditate on a favorite verse about patience (perhaps James 5:7–8). Write it on a 3 x 5 card and post it on your bathroom mirror.

☐ The next time you find yourself getting impatient, take a time out.

☐ Go over your personal calendar and see if you are trying to do too much in too little time. Eliminate one unnecessary activity.

☐ Plant a seed and wait for it to sprout.

Things to Remember

My friends, be patient until the Lord returns. Think of farmers who wait patiently for the spring and summer rains to make their valuable crops grow. Be patient like those farmers and don't give up.

JAMES 5:7–8 CEV

Be glad for all God is planning for you. Be patient in trouble, and always be prayerful.

ROMANS 12:12 NLT

Jesus said, "In your patience possess your souls."

LUKE 21:19 NKJV

After he had patiently endured, he obtained the promise.

HEBREWS 6:15 NKJV

Be still before the LORD, and wait patiently for him, do not fret over those who prosper in their way, over those who carry out evil devices.

PSALM 37:7 NRSV

I waited patiently for the LORD; and He inclined to me, and heard my cry.

PSALM 40:1 NKJV

Teach us, O Lord, the disciplines of patience, for to wait is often harder than to work.

—PETER MARSHALL

On every level of life from housework to the heights of prayer, in all judgement and all efforts to get things done, hurry and impatience are the sure marks of an amateur.

—EVELYN UNDERHILL

Checklist for Life *for* Men

God is to us like the sky to a small bird, which cannot see its outer limits and cannot reach its distant horizons, but can only lose itself in the greatness and immensity of the blueness.

> —John Powell

Can you fathom the mysteries of God? Can you probe the limits of the Almighty? They are higher than the heavens—what can you do? Their measure is longer than the earth and wider than the sea.

> —Job 11:7–9 NIV

Boldness

Go Boldly Where No Man Has Gone Before

Do not throw away this confident trust in the Lord, no matter what happens. Remember the great reward it brings you!

—HEBREWS 10:35 NLT

Men were created to live dangerous, adventurous lives, to live boldly in everything they do. You know this because you know that God created you in His image, and He is all powerful. In fact the Bible says that "Warrior" is His name.

Does that mean that you can do and say whatever you want and say to others, "If you don't like it, tough"? God does not want you to be a bully—even a spiritual bully. Jesus, when He was on earth, was tough when He had to be; He didn't back down from anyone. He was no wimp, but He also did not go around intimidating others or bossing them around. He was loving and caring, and he lived from a servant's heart.

The degrees that you may earn, the number of years that you may attain in your career, and the higher tax bracket that you may reach are all good signs in your life, but true confidence is inherited. True confidence comes from the spiritual genes passed on to you by your heavenly Father. Living boldly is nothing more than knowing who you are as a child of God and understanding how He wants to use you.

If you're a salesman, sell boldly! Don't approach a potential deal with doubt in your mind. Talk with the person as if you expect the transaction to happen. If you have to give a presentation at a meeting, present boldly! Prepare more than you need to, stand tall and straight in front of your audience, and speak clearly and with authority, conviction, and passion. Whatever you do, wherever you go, act like the ambassador of almighty God that you are.

What about when you don't feel all that bold? Circumstances may come your way where you feel that you don't have what it takes—that maybe you should just step aside and wait until things get easier. Don't listen to that lie! Open your Bible and read some of the apostle Paul's letters. He was faced with all kinds of oppositions and threats against his life, yet he did not back down. And when you think you cannot go it alone, turn to your fellow brothers in Christ and go into battle together.

Thank God for filling you with His strength and confidence, which He gives to you abundantly if you seek to live your life as a reflection of Him.

I Will

See myself as a godly warrior and not as a religious wimp.

yes _____ *no* _____

Believe that I was created in the image of the almighty God.

yes _____ *no* _____

Recognize God as the source of my strength.

yes _____ *no* _____

Approach each day looking for opportunities to win rather than looking for ways to simply survive.

yes _____ *no* _____

Align myself with other men who are living courageous lives for God.

yes _____ *no* _____

Keep hope at the front of my mind at all times, expecting to be victorious through God's strength.

yes _____ *no* _____

Things to Do

☐ *Make a list of all of your strengths.*

☐ *On the same sheet of paper, write down your weaknesses, greatest to smallest.*

☐ *Cross out the weaknesses over which you have no control or those insignificant to your pursuit of spiritual valor, and circle the weaknesses that you know you could transform into strengths.*

☐ *Count up the number of current or projected strengths and compare that number to those you crossed out.*

☐ *Take your smallest weakness and pray about it—ask God to give you opportunities to work on it and the strength to face it head-on.*

☐ *Talk to a close friend or two and ask them to be your allies in your battle to live life boldly in this one area.*

Things to Remember

The LORD is my strength and song, and He has become my salvation.

PSALM 118:14 NKJV

He is my God, and I will praise Him; my father's God, and I will exalt Him.

EXODUS 15:2 NKJV

You, LORD, have made me glad through Your work; I will triumph in the works of Your hands.

PSALM 92:4 NKJV

I saw God before me for all time. Nothing can shake me; he's right by my side. I'm glad from the inside out, ecstatic; I've pitched my tent in the land of hope.

ACTS 2:26 THE MESSAGE

I will not be afraid of ten thousands of people who have set themselves against me all around.

PSALM 3:6 NKJV

God has not given us a spirit of fear, but of power and of love and of a sound mind.

2 TIMOTHY 1:7 NKJV

You have confidence in yourself, which is valuable, if not an indispensable quality.

—ABRAHAM LINCOLN

I place no hope in my strength, nor in my works: but all my confidence is in God my protector, who never abandons those who have put all their hope and thought in him.

—FRANÇOIS RABELAIS

Commitment

Seeing Things Through

Jesus said, "He who endures to the end shall be saved."

—Matthew 24:13 NKJV

Watch a televised marathon, and you'll see an interesting phenomenon. As the starter gun fires, a few novice runners will sprint to the front of the pack. Those attention-grabbers will enjoy a few moments on camera, but it is unlikely that they will cross the finish line twenty-six-plus miles later. Finishing a marathon requires patience, perspective, endurance, strength, and just plain grit. It's a lot like life.

You can bring a champion marathoner's commitment to your life's goals—ensuring that you will start fresh and finish strong—by following the three *P*s: preparation, perspective, and perseverence.

Preparation. The early breakout sprinters from the first paragraph couldn't finish the race they started so briskly because they weren't prepared for the long challenge ahead of them. Perhaps they didn't train well or formulate a race plan to ensure they were mentally ready.

Don't make that mistake. Prepare yourself to achieve

your goals. For example, if you want to lose fifteen pounds, prepare yourself by reading what qualified people have to say about the subject. Talk with family members or friends who have been successful shedding weight and keeping it off. Enlist their support.

Perspective. A marathoner realizes that he has a long race before him. He doesn't get caught up in the early excitement and expend too much energy at the beginning. He paces himself.

You can do the same thing. For example, if you decide to get an advanced degree, pace yourself. Don't take too many classes up-front. And don't try to read all your text materials in the first month.

Perspective can also help you at the middle or near the end of your endeavor. When a marathoner hits the midpoint of his race, he can tell himself, *I don't even have to run a marathon any more—only a half marathon!*

Perseverance. Any goal will present obstacles and disappointments. Even with all the preparation and perspective in the world, you may reach a point of mental and physical fatigue as you strive to finish what you've started.

Times like these require perseverance. Willpower. Determination. Grit. Remind yourself what your goal is, how much it means to you, and how you will feel if you don't achieve it.

You might not have the stamina of an elite marathon runner, but you can match his or her determination. And when you finish what you've begun, you can share in the triumph.

I Will

Stay focused on, and committed to, my key life goals.

yes _no_

Be patient as I strive to achieve my goals.

yes _no_

Avoid letting fatigue, self-doubt, or criticism from others trip me up as I strive to fulfill ambitions.

yes _no_

Share my goals with God and ask Him for the wisdom and the will to achieve them.

yes _no_

Build and maintain strong relationships with people who can help me achieve my goals.

yes _no_

Always note the progress I have made toward accomplishing what I set out to do.

yes _no_

Things to Do

☐ _Write down a major life goal and a timetable for achieving it._

☐ _Share your goal with a friend or family member and ask him or her to help keep you accountable._

☐ _Celebrate with this person every time you make a significant step toward your goal._

☐ _Read an article by or about someone who has achieved a goal similar to yours._

☐ _Read the first chapter of James to get God's perspective on perseverance and commitment._

☐ _Make a list of possible obstacles along the pathway toward your goal and devise a plan for overcoming or eliminating them._

Things to Remember

May the God of all grace, who called us to His eternal glory by Christ Jesus, after you have suffered a while, perfect, establish, strengthen, and settle you.

1 PETER 5:10 NKJV

Our light affliction, which is but for a moment, is working for us a far more exceeding and eternal weight of glory.

2 CORINTHIANS 4:17 NKJV

Jesus said, "Which of you, intending to build a tower, does not sit down first and count the cost, whether he has enough to finish it."

LUKE 14:28 NKJV

The Lord GOD will help Me; therefore I will not be disgraced; therefore I have set My face like a flint, and I know that I will not be ashamed.

ISAIAH 50:7 NKJV

Be strong and do not let your hands be weak, for your work shall be rewarded!

2 CHRONICLES 15:7 NKJV

He will give eternal life to everyone who has patiently done what is good in the hope of receiving glory, honor, and life that lasts forever.

ROMANS 2:7 CEV

The person who makes a success of living is the one who sees his goal steadily and aims for it unswervingly. That is dedication.
—CECIL B. DEMILLE

The profundity of a spiritual act is in direct proportion to its author's commitment.
—HENRI DE LUBAC

Your Actions Lead Better Than Words

The LORD said to Joshua, "No man shall be able to stand before you all the days of your life: as I was with Moses, so I will be with you. I will not leave you nor forsake you."

—JOSHUA 1:5 NKJV

John Wooden is a college basketball legend. During his years at UCLA, his teams won a host of national titles. Losses were rare for Wooden's Bruins, and he coached many players, including Bill Walton and Kareem Abdul-Jabbar, who went on to become NBA superstars.

Many factors contributed to Wooden's success. He was a student of the game. He had an eye for talent. He was a great motivator.

However, when former players talk about the privilege of playing for Coach Wooden, they reveal the true key to his effectiveness as a leader: He led by example. One of his most famous axioms was "I never ask a player to do anything—during a game or in practice—that I haven't done myself." Because of this, his players knew that any drills Coach Wooden put them through were for their benefit, and that he wasn't asking them to do something impossible.

Wooden didn't order his players to maintain their composure during games while he screamed at officials, threw chairs, or manhandled a confused point guard. He was an intense competitor, but he didn't let his intensity make him do something foolish that would embarrass him or cost his team a game.

Ben Franklin was another wise man who understood that an ounce of leading by example was worth ten pounds of leading by pressure and intimidation. At one point in his life, Franklin wanted his city, Philadelphia, to lighten up. He believed that lighting the city's streets would not only improve the town aesthetically but also make it safer. But he didn't try to persuade Philly's citizens by talking to them. Instead, he hung a beautiful lantern near his front door. He kept the lantern brightly polished and carefully and faithfully lit the wick each evening just before dusk.

People strolling the dark street saw Franklin's light from a long way off. They found its glow to be friendly and beautiful—and a helpful, guiding landmark. Soon, Franklin's neighbors began placing lanterns in front of their own homes. Before long, the whole city was dotted with light, and more and more people began to appreciate the beauty and value of Franklin's bright idea.

Just as Franklin and Wooden became points of light, your actions can become beacons for those around you—children, employees, fellow church members, and so on. What they see, they copy. And when they see the light of your good example, they may be inspired to illuminate a candle of their own.

I Will

Remember that leadership is more about action than mere rhetoric.   *yes*   *no*

Strive to be a consistent, reliable example to those I wish to lead.   *yes*   *no*

Emulate the character of great religious, business, and political leaders.   *yes*   *no*

Weigh my leadership decisions against the Bible to make sure they are sound and pleasing to God.   *yes*   *no*

Be a humble leader, never taking my authority for granted or abusing it.   *yes*   *no*

Confess my mistakes, realizing that this honesty will build my credibility with those I lead.   *yes*   *no*

Things to Do

- [ ] *Memorize Colossians 4:1 (NKJV)—"Masters, give your bondservants what is just and fair, knowing that you also have a Master in heaven."*

- [ ] *Read the Gospel of John and note the attributes that made Jesus such an effective leader.*

- [ ] *Keep a leadership journal, chronicling your leadership successes and setbacks.*

- [ ] *Create a checklist of the qualities of a great leader; measure yourself against this list periodically.*

- [ ] *Thank God for providing His Son, a beautiful example of servant leadership.*

- [ ] *During the next year, attend a workshop or symposium on leadership.*

Things to Remember

Jesus said, "You are the light of the world. . . . Let your light so shine before men, that they may see your good works and glorify your Father in heaven."

MATTHEW 5:14, 16 NKJV

Jesus said, "Whoever desires to become great among you shall be your servant. And whoever of you desires to be first shall be slave of all. For even the Son of Man did not come to be served, but to serve, and to give His life a ransom for many."

MARK 10:43–45 NKJV

A man is known by his actions. An evil man lives an evil life; a good man lives a godly life.

PROVERBS 21:8 TLB

Let us stop just saying we love people; let us really love them, and show it by our actions.

1 JOHN 3:18 TLB

Christ . . . is your example. Follow in his steps: He never sinned, never told a lie, never answered back when insulted; when he suffered he did not threaten to get even; he left his case in the hands of God who always judges fairly.

1 PETER 2:20–22 TLB

> True greatness, true leadership, is achieved not by reducing men to one's service but in giving oneself in selfless service to them.
>
> —OSWALD SANDERS

> Although potential leaders are born, effective leaders are made.
>
> —BENNIE E. GOODWIN

Become the Richest Man in the World

On the first day of every week, each one of you should set aside a sum of money in keeping with his income, saving it up, so that when I come no collections will have to be made.

—1 CORINTHIANS 16:2 NIV

Open the pages of a men's magazine and note what's being advertised: luxury cars, sports cars, digital TVs, computers that fit in the palm of your hand, plastic surgery, thousand-dollar suits, Swiss watches.

Many American men, it seems, have a possession obsession. And while there's nothing inherently wrong with wanting fine clothes, state-of-the-art business accessories, or cool sports equipment, material goods can easily become a source of false security, even pride.

The same danger exists with money. Many men strive to earn bonuses, get maximum profit sharing, and beef up their 401k accounts. "More" never seems to be "enough." Are you satisfied with your present earnings? Do they cover all your expenses? Are you able to save as much for the future as you'd like? Or do you crave a substantial raise and hope to get to the next level, the next plateau on Money Mountain?

The ultimate test of your success in life is not how much wealth and possessions you can amass. On the contrary, Jesus taught His followers to travel light, taking with them only what they would need for their journey. He reminded them to concentrate on God's divine love, which provides a richness unmatched by any worldly possession. This love is so brilliant that it makes everything else pale in comparison. Materialism, on the other hand, is excess baggage that in the end only serves to make the journey burdensome.

To help them travel light, Jesus taught His followers to give. When we give to others out of our time, money, and resources, Jesus says that we are giving to Him—not *as if* we are giving to Him, but in fact are giving to Him.

Do you want to become a truly rich man? Don't encumber yourself with possessions you don't need. Don't be consumed with getting to the next tax bracket. Focus on traveling light and giving freely. After all, material possessions can be stolen or destroyed. Retirement funds can shrink. Jobs can be lost.

But the caring and compassion that you give to others can make a lasting impact. A few people may be impressed by or envious of a man's material wealth. Their lives, however, can be deeply enriched by his generosity.

Think about your life's goals and priorities. Do you want to be known or remembered for how much you saved or for how much you gave?

I Will

Remind myself often that all I have, or ever will have, has come from God.

yes _____ *no* _____

Strive to develop a thankful heart, by taking time each day to thank God for all He has given me, both materially and spiritually.

yes _____ *no* _____

Focus on what I truly need in life, not what I want.

yes _____ *no* _____

Seek God's wisdom as I evaluate my purchases and investment decisions.

yes _____ *no* _____

Avoid comparing my salary, home, car, etc., to someone else's.

yes _____ *no* _____

Ask God to forgive me for the times I have let greed creep into my heart.

yes _____ *no* _____

Things to Do

☐ *Conduct a personal financial audit to determine what percentage of your discretionary income is going to charity.*

☐ *Do a thorough spring cleaning of your residence (even if it's not spring). Collect unneeded items to donate to a local charity or school.*

☐ *Memorize Hebrews 13:5 (NKJV)—"Let your conduct be without covetousness; be content with such things as you have."*

☐ *Within the next year, attend a biblically based workshop on financial management.*

☐ *Read the book of Ecclesiastes and note Solomon's ultimate verdict on material wealth.*

☐ *Write a note of encouragement to someone you see giving to others in a Christ-like manner.*

Things to Remember

Jesus said to them, "Take heed and beware of covetousness, for one's life does not consist in the abundance of the things he possesses."

LUKE 12:15 NKJV

Let each one give as he purposes in his heart, not grudgingly or of necessity; for God loves a cheerful giver.

2 CORINTHIANS 9:7 NKJV

"Bring all the tithes into the storehouse, that there may be food in My house, and try Me now in this," says the LORD of hosts, "If I will not open for you the windows of heaven and pour out for you such blessing that there will not be room enough to receive it."

MALACHI 3:10 NKJV

Honor the LORD with your possessions, and with the firstfruits of all your increase; so your barns will be filled with plenty, and your vats will overflow with new wine.

PROVERBS 3:9–10 NKJV

The love of money is a root of all kinds of evil, for which some have strayed from the faith in their greediness, and pierced themselves through with many sorrows.

1 TIMOTHY 6:10 NKJV

God made man to be somebody, not just to have things.
—AUTHOR UNKNOWN

If a person gets his attitude toward money straight, it will help straighten out almost every other area in his life.
—BILLY GRAHAM

Do You Know Who You Are?

Put on the new man, which was created according to God, in true righteousness and holiness.

—EPHESIANS 4:24 NKJV

A man with what he thought was an amazing replica of a Leonardo da Vinci painting took his work of art to a museum. He showed the copied painting to the curator to get his reaction. The curator immediately identified the painting as a forgery—and also hypothesized about the identity of the copyist, his nationality, and when the copy was made.

Then the curator turned the painting over. The information on the back confirmed that he was right on all three counts. "How did you know it was a fake?" the man asked. "It looks like an amazing likeness to me."

"People who make a living copying the masters have little imagination of their own," the curator explained. "And this person's choice of subject, brush strokes, and areas of emphasis practically scream 'Fake!' Think about those celebrity impersonators, how they overemphasize a certain vocal inflection, facial expression, or gesture. It's the same thing here."

Whatever your calling in life, you may be tempted to copy the successful people in your field. But the best one can hope for with this approach is the moniker Master Imitator, not Master Artist, Musician, Writer, or whatever. True, many take the well-traveled path; that's why we have six *Police Academy* movies and only one *Casablanca*. But this road doesn't lead to greatness or pride in one's work.

If you truly want to distinguish yourself, be an innovator, not an imitator. God has given you unique skills, ideas, and experiences. There is no one just like you anywhere on the planet. Take some time to think about the characteristics that make you, you! Write them down on a piece of paper and keep it with you. Work on only one characteristic at a time. If it is a positive quality—something you like about yourself— ask God to help you find new ways to nurture and express it. Then seek out opportunities to exercise that trait in the service of others.

If the quality is something you would consider negative— something you dislike about yourself—ask God to show you how to turn a liability into an asset. For example, if you have trouble being still, ask God to help you seek out opportunities to use your extra energy to help others.

Most of all, remember that there's only one way to be a true original in this copycat world: Be yourself.

I Will

Strive to maintain my individuality, resisting the
pressure to conform.   *yes*   *no*

Thank God for making me a unique creation.

Do and say what is right and true, not necessarily
what is popular or trendy.   *yes*   *no*

Pray for the courage to be an individual.   *yes*   *no*

Periodically check my speech, dress, and behavior to
ensure I'm avoiding conformity.   *yes*   *no*

Make a point to warn the children in my life about
the dangers of nameless, faceless conformity and
encourage them to live out and celebrate their
unique God-given gifts.   *yes*   *no*

Things to Do

☐ *Memorize Ephesians 2:10 (NKJV)—"We are His workmanship, created in
Christ Jesus for good works, which God prepared beforehand that we
should walk in them."*

☐ *Read an article by or about a strong, unique individual you admire.*

☐ *Make a list of the positive qualities that make you an individual and
separate you from the pack. Check yourself against this list at least
once a year.*

☐ *Read Romans 12:1–8 for a biblical model of individuality.*

☐ *Ask your spouse or a trusted friend about what makes you a true
individual in his or her eyes—then work on building these traits.*

Things to Remember

In Him we live and move and have
our being.

ACTS 17:28 NKJV

We are His workmanship, created in
Christ Jesus for good works, which God
prepared beforehand that we should
walk in them.

EPHESIANS 2:10 NKJV

There are diversities of gifts, but the
same Spirit. There are differences of
ministries, but the same Lord. And there
are diversities of activities, but it is the
same God who works all in all.

1 CORINTHIANS 12:4–6 NKJV

Just as there are many parts to our
bodies, so it is with Christ's body. We
are all parts of it, and it takes every one
of us to make it complete, for we each
have different work to do. So we belong
to each other, and each needs all
the others.

ROMANS 12:5 TLB

You formed my inward parts; You
covered me in my mother's womb. I will
praise You, for I am fearfully and
wonderfully made; marvelous are Your
works, and that my soul knows
very well.

PSALM 139:13–14 NKJV

Be what you are.
This is the first
step toward
becoming better
than you are.

—JULIUS CHARLES HARE
AND AUGUSTUS WILLIAM
HARE

Meeting people
unlike oneself does
not enlarge one's
outlook; it only
confirms one's idea
that one is unique.

—ELIZABETH BOWEN

Your Grass Is Really the Greenest

Serving God does make us very rich, if we are satisfied with what we have.

—1 TIMOTHY 6:6 NCV

Most men are competitive at their core. The reason is twofold: One, men love to win; and, two, men hate to lose. Competition is more an issue of contentment than it is a pursuit of victory—a man doesn't want the competition to possess what he doesn't have. Can you relate? But consider this. If God has placed you where He wants you to be and given you what He wants you to have, then perhaps you need to be content and not worry about the other guy.

As you get older, competition shifts from the sports field to the grassy field of your backyard. Sure, you may enjoy working out in the yard, but you may also be motivated by dissatisfaction with the condition of your lawn. You may find yourself believing the cliché that the grass is greener on the other side of the fence. But that couldn't really be true. Right?

Is the grass greener on the other side of the fence? According to James Pomerantz in his scientific article "'The Grass Is Always Greener': An Ecological Analysis of an Old [Saying]" (Perception, 1983), optical and perceptual laws alone can make the neighbor's lawn look greener than the blades of grass perpendicular to the ground that one looks down upon in his own yard.

It's hard to find contentment in your life when you spend too much time looking at what other people have. When that happens, you soon only see what you lack rather than what you are blessed with. That is one of Satan's favorite ploys. One, he wants to pit you against your brothers, and, two, he wants to shift your eyes off what God has done and is doing in your life.

So how can you get past this green-grass fabrication? One thing you can do is to figuratively tear down the fences between you and your neighbors and spend time with each other. See them as allies rather than as rivals. Another thing you can do is to enjoy the grass in your yard. Unless God provides the rain and sun (i.e., unless He wants you to have something you don't right now), then don't worry about it. Ask God to open your eyes to what you have and to give you a spirit of contentment with the beautiful grass under your feet.

I Will

Feel richly blessed because what God has given me.	*yes*	*no*
Stop complaining or obsessing over what I don't have.	*yes*	*no*
Believe that God blesses me daily with things that go unnoticed.	*yes*	*no*
Be happy for my neighbor and not envious.	*yes*	*no*
See my neighbor as my ally rather than as my enemy.	*yes*	*no*
Stop competing and start enjoying life.	*yes*	*no*
Know that God withholds some blessings for very good reasons.	*yes*	*no*

Things to Do

☐ *Walk barefoot on your lawn, feeling the blades between your toes and noticing the lush green colors.*

☐ *Walk over to your neighbor's yard and see how similar it is to yours.*

☐ *Write down things you don't have but wish you did (talents, material possessions, spiritual gifts).*

☐ *Pray about those things on your list, and cross them off one by one as you give them over to God, knowing that He will give them to you in His perfect time if He wants you to have them.*

☐ *Walk around your house and thank God for at least ten things He has blessed you with (in your home or your heart).*

☐ *Take a day off work just to relax at home—don't go anywhere and don't do any chores.*

Things to Remember

I have learned how to get along happily whether I have much or little.

PHILIPPIANS 4:11 TLB

Remove falsehood and lies far from me; give me neither poverty nor riches—feed me with the food allotted to me.

PROVERBS 30:8 NKJV

Let your conduct be without covetousness; be content with such things as you have. For He Himself has said, "I will never leave you nor forsake you."

HEBREWS 13:5 NKJV

Better is a little with the fear of the LORD, than great treasure with trouble.

PROVERBS 15:16 NKJV

A little that a righteous man has is better than the riches of many wicked.

PSALM 37:16 NKJV

Again, I saw that for all toil and every skillful work a man is envied by his neighbor. This also is vanity and grasping for the wind.

ECCLESIASTES 4:4 NKJV

To be content is to be happy.
—CHINESE PROVERB

Little I ask; my wants are few, I only want a hut of stone, (A very plain brownstone will do,) That I may call my own.
—OLIVER WENDELL HOLMES

Your Name Is on a Trophy

*Thanks be to God, who gives us the victory through our Lord
Jesus Christ.*

—1 Corinthians 15:57 NKJV

God is always victorious. Nothing is too difficult for
Him. And what's more, with His help, you can be
victorious too. He can lead you through to victory over
any problem, issue, or struggle in your life.

While this may be easy to accept on the surface, it can
be much more difficult to believe when you are in the
midst of a really difficult situation. Perhaps you have a
mountain of debt and wonder how you will ever be able
to get out from under it. Or you may be ill or struggling
with the illness of a loved one or friend. Do you feel like
giving up under the pressure? Is there a difficult person in
your life? Are you dealing with problems in your marriage?
In your work? With your children? It's easy to become
discouraged. But God wants you to lean on Him and let
Him show you how to be a winner in every situation
you encounter.

In the Bible, David found himself in the midst of just such a daunting challenge when he went up against a giant named Goliath. Goliath was a nine-foot-tall champion fighter who wore 125 pounds of armor and wielded a 15-pound javelin. David was a scrawny shepherd boy who probably wore goatskins and carried a slingshot. For all intents and purposes, David was completely outclassed, and Goliath should have squashed him like a bug.

However, David already knew that God had given him the victory, so when his fellow Israelites tried to dress him in heavy armor for protection, he refused it and placed his trust in God's protection. And this is what you should do when you face a seemingly impossible situation. Stop relying on your own effort and put your trust in God, for He wants you to succeed and triumph in all you do. Victory will come at a price (you'll have to work for it), and it may not come right away (you'll have to be patient), but it will come. Above all, don't focus so hard on the present problem that you miss all the other victories God gives you every day!

Step onto that battlefield just like David did and go forward with the tools God has given you—even if that means zinging a pebble at your giant. When God is in control of the situation, that little pebble will hit the problem right on the head and knock it down flat. Your feeble weapons are mighty in God's hands.

I Will

Realize that God is always victorious.   _yes_ _no_

Believe that God will give me victory.   _yes_ _no_

Remember all the little victories God gives me
each day.   _yes_ _no_

Remain confident even when I feel defeated.   _yes_ _no_

View challenges as an opportunity for victory,
not defeat.   _yes_ _no_

Believe that God is with me in my struggles.   _yes_ _no_

Trust that God will show me the way to victory.   _yes_ _no_

Things to Do

☐ Make a list of at least five victories that God has given you
in the past year.

☐ Look for the little victories that God gives you each day.

☐ Pick out one area of your life where you have a struggle and need
victory, then give it to God in prayer.

☐ Read the story of David and Goliath in 1 Samuel 17.

☐ Talk to a friend about a failure you are experiencing and ask him to
pray about it.

☐ Read a story about someone who overcame great odds to win victory,
such as that of Joan of Arc (victory in battle) or Stephen Hawking
(victory over physical disability).

Things to Remember

The weapons of our warfare are not carnal but mighty in God for pulling down strongholds.

2 CORINTHIANS 10:4 NKJV

Oh, sing to the LORD a new song! For He has done marvelous things; His right hand and His holy arm have gained Him the victory.

PSALM 98:1 NKJV

Whatever is born of God overcomes the world. And this is the victory that has overcome the world—our faith.

1 JOHN 5:4 NKJV

Do you not know that those who run in a race all run, but one receives the prize? Run in such a way that you may obtain it.

1 CORINTHIANS 9:24 NKJV

Oh, clap your hands, all you peoples! Shout to God with the voice of triumph!

PSALM 47:1 NKJV

Thanks be to God who always leads us in triumph in Christ, and through us diffuses the fragrance of His knowledge in every place.

2 CORINTHIANS 2:14 NKJV

If Christ is with us, who is against us? You can fight with confidence where you are sure of victory. With Christ and for Christ victory is certain.

—SAINT BERNARD OF CLAIRVAUX

God wants us to be victors, not victims; to grow, not grovel; to soar; not sink; to overcome, not to be overwhelmed.

—WILLIAM ARTHUR WARD

Give God His Due

Give to the LORD the glory due His name; bring an offering, and come before Him. Oh, worship the LORD in the beauty of holiness!

—1 CHRONICLES 16:29 NKJV

Humans were created to worship—it's a basic instinct that dwells within every person. So strong is that inner urging, that if you don't worship God, you will seek out some other person or object to focus your affections on. The Bible refers to those other things as "idols," and they have always been a stumbling block for believers.

In the Old Testament, when Moses went up to Mount Sinai and didn't return for forty days, the Israelites melted down their jewelry and made a golden calf to worship. When God brought them into the Promised Land, they started worshiping a god called Baal.

In the New Testament, idol worship was so prevalent that Paul had to caution the Corinthian Christians not to eat food offered to them. And in 1 John 5:21, John felt compelled to write, "Little children, keep yourselves from idols" (NKJV).

The idols that people serve today are not images made

of metal, wood, or stone, but things like careers, activities, interests, relationships, possessions—anything that comes before God in their lives. Have you ever considered whether there may be idols in your life?

God knows that pursuing such idols can lead to feelings of emptiness. He knows the disappointment you will experience if you place your trust in them. That is why He wants you to focus your worship on Him; He will never fail you.

So check out your heart. Are there any idols on the throne of your life? Do you worship anyone or anything other than God? And remember that worship is more than saying prescribed words and expressions. It is also the devotion you show to someone or something as shown through your actions, attitudes, and priorities.

If your answer is no, you are probably already aware of the benefits of worshiping God by putting Him first in your life. If your answer is yes, it's never too late to lay aside your idols and turn your praise and worship to God alone. As you center your life on Him, you will begin to actively experience His love, and you will want to direct that love outwardly in service toward others. You will receive His wisdom and guidance to help you in everything you do, and you will receive His power and protection. Best of all, you will receive joy and fulfillment in life that only God can give.

I Will

Believe God is worthy of worship. _yes_ _no_

Accept that if I don't worship God, I worship
other things. _yes_ _no_

Realize that the way I live my life can be a form of
worship. _yes_ _no_

Maintain my relationship with God through worship. _yes_ _no_

Trust that worshiping God leads to fulfillment. _yes_ _no_

Allow God to show me the idols I have set up
in my life. _yes_ _no_

Experience God's love through worship. _yes_ _no_

Things to Do

☐ *Spend a few minutes thanking and praising God.*

☐ *List five to ten idols in your life that you often put before God.*

☐ *Write out a plan for how you will eliminate false idols in your life.*
Start with the phrase, "I will put God first by . . ."

☐ *Read one of the following psalms of worship each morning for the next*
week: Psalms 8, 9, 18, 23, 66, 81, 96.

☐ *Ask God to help you live a life of devotion to Him.*

☐ *Sing a hymn of worship in your quiet time with God.*

☐ *Think of one or two things that you can do for another person in the*
next few weeks as an act of worship to God.

Things to Remember

Give unto the LORD the glory due to His name; worship the LORD in the beauty of holiness.

PSALM 29:2 NKJV

You must worship no other gods, but only Jehovah, for he is a God who claims absolute loyalty and exclusive devotion.

EXODUS 34:14 TLB

Jesus said, "The hour is coming, and now is, when the true worshipers will worship the Father in spirit and truth; for the Father is seeking such to worship Him. God is Spirit, and those who worship Him must worship in spirit and truth."

JOHN 4:23–24 NKJV

Oh come, let us worship and bow down; let us kneel before the LORD our Maker. For He is our God, and we are the people of His pasture, and the sheep of His hand.

PSALM 95:6–7 NKJV

Who shall not fear You, O Lord, and glorify Your name? For You alone are holy. For all nations shall come and worship before You, for Your judgments have been manifested.

REVELATION 15:4 NKJV

We may be truly said to worship God, though we lack perfection; but we cannot be said to worship Him if we lack sincerity.

—STEPHEN CHARNOCK

Worship is the highest and noblest activity of which man, by the grace of God, is capable.

—JOHN STOTT

Life Is a Marathon, Not a Sprint

Let us hold fast the confession of our hope without wavering, for He who promised is faithful.

—HEBREWS 10:23 NKJV

The apostle Paul compared a person living a godly life to that of an athlete running a race. Like the athlete who must train hard to have physical stamina to finish the race that he is running, the man who wishes to live a life pleasing to God must train hard to have spiritual stamina. He must have perseverance.

Perseverance means trusting God and consistently following His ways because you know that He will stand beside you and help get you through the toughest times in life. The remarkable thing about perseverance is that it makes you focus on the prize rather than on the obstacles that stand in your way. When you focus on the reward and think about all the incredible things God has promised you when this life is over, you can't help but be optimistic about the future.

It's easy when you first turn your life over to God to dive headlong into the Bible and spend hours in prayer in order to grow in the Lord as quickly as possible. That's a good thing, but you must remember that as time passes, the excitement will fade somewhat and the newness of your experience will wear off. It takes time and patience and commitment to develop godly character. But, as so many have discovered before you, including the apostle Paul, it will be worth it when you hear God say, "Well done." So don't let yourself get winded after the first sprint and give up. Stay in the race until you have won the prize.

It is important to remember that life is a marathon, not a sprint, and that there are things you can do to develop perseverance. Start off small by developing daily habits like reading a few chapters from the Bible or spending a few minutes in prayer. Don't try to do too much at once or give up at the first sign of failure. Try to fellowship with other people who have a relationship with God when you can, for through them you will gain support and encouragement. When you finally have time to look back at the course at the end, you will be amazed at how far you have come and be glad you stayed the course.

Everyone who crosses the finish line of that race gets the prize. The important thing is that you get there.

I Will

Accept the fact that living a life for God requires perseverance.

yes   _no_

Allow God to strengthen me when I am weary and want to give up.

yes   _no_

View life as a marathon, not as a sprint.

yes   _no_

Believe that God will help me to persevere.

yes   _no_

Exhibit patience and commitment in my life.

yes   _no_

Remember that God's schedule for my spiritual growth is often different from my own.

yes   _no_

Trust that God will bring others into my life to give me support and encouragement.

yes   _no_

Things to Do

☐ _Share a personal struggle with a friend or spouse and ask them to help you persevere._

☐ _Make a personal commitment to develop habits that will help you persevere in your relationship with God (such as attending church regularly or spending time each day reading the Bible)._

☐ _Write out a prayer asking God to help you persevere in living a life that is pleasing to Him._

☐ _Look for and encourage someone who is struggling to endure some hardship or overcome a bad habit._

☐ _Watch the 1993 movie_ Rudy _about perseverance and determination in the face of overwhelming obstacles._

Things to Remember

My beloved brethren, be steadfast, immovable, always abounding in the work of the Lord, knowing that your labor is not in vain in the Lord.

1 Corinthians 15:58 NKJV

In the Parable of the Talents, Jesus said, "His lord said to him, 'Well done, good and faithful servant; you were faithful over a few things, I will make you ruler over many things. Enter into the joy of your lord.'"

Matthew 25:21 NKJV

We desire that each one of you show the same diligence to the full assurance of hope until the end, that you do not become sluggish, but imitate those who through faith and patience inherit the promises.

Hebrews 6:11–12 NKJV

Let us not grow weary while doing good, for in due season we shall reap if we do not lose heart.

Galatians 6:9 NKJV

We have become partakers of Christ if we hold the beginning of our confidence steadfast to the end.

Hebrews 3:14 NKJV

Perseverance is the sister of patience, the daughter of constancy, the friend of peace, the cementer of friendships, the bond of harmony and bulwark of holiness.

—Bernard of Clairvaux

Perseverance is not a long race; it is many short races one after another.

—Dr. V. Raymond Edman

Don't Always Take Life So Seriously

To everything there is a season, a time for every purpose under heaven.

—ECCLESIASTES 3:1 NKJV

A man's responsibilities can take up almost every waking moment. Balancing the demands of a career and oftentimes a family can leave even the strongest man feeling washed out and overwhelmed. But all work and no play can be damaging and counterproductive. Even the busiest man needs to set aside a little time for fun—time to laugh and shrug off your worries, time to relax your muscles and loosen your nerves, time to recover your balance and regain your perspective.

If you're like most men, you may actually feel guilty about having fun when there are still so many things to do. But taking time for play is not, as many believe, a worthless pursuit. Even twenty minutes shooting hoops in the driveway or running your dog on the beach or shooting a round of pool in the rec room at work can help you dump tension, unlock creativity, and rekindle energy.

Would you be surprised to hear that fun can also improve your spiritual life? Did you think that God and fun just don't mix? Consider for a moment that God created your sense of humor right along with your sense of responsibility. He wants you to exercise both. He knows that all fun and no responsibility will leave you feeling empty and hopeless, but all responsibility and no fun will make you brittle, legalistic, and embittered.

Chances are that Jesus had some fun with His disciples. He shared meals with them and traveled with them. It's unlikely that every moment of every day was spent in deep reflection and meditation. They made friends and touched lives along the way.

What types of things do you enjoy doing? What activities do you consider fun? Do you like to play with your kids? Hunt or fish? Swim or workout? Engage in some sport? Take in a movie? Read? Tackle a crossword puzzle? Take a few minutes to think of two activities you would love to engage in if you just had the time. Then make time. You will be shocked to find that a twenty-minute break in the morning can actually facilitate a 5:00 p.m. deadline.

If you are one of those men who take a fun break on a regular basis, feel good about it. Congratulate yourself for being smarter than the average bear. If you aren't taking time to play, it's time to wise up! You'll be better off for it.

I Will

Look for the fun in life.

yes *no*

Resolve to include fun in my daily routines.

yes *no*

Carefully reflect before taking on new
responsibilities.

yes *no*

Try to be more spontaneous.

yes *no*

Recognize that God wants me to live a
balanced life.

yes *no*

Thank God for the ability to enjoy my life.

yes *no*

Encourage another person to take time away from
the daily grind and have some fun.

yes *no*

Things to Do

☐ *Think back to some activity you did that was fun and do it again.*

☐ *Make a list of what you consider to be enjoyable things to do.*

☐ *Plan to leave work early one day and spend it doing whatever seems like fun to you.*

☐ *Turn your cell phone off for a few hours and don't feel guilty about it!*

☐ *Play a game with your kids, family, or friends.*

☐ *Turn a task at your work into a game to make it fun.*

☐ *Treat a coworker, family member, or friend to a fun time—coffee, bowling, movie, sports, golfing, fishing, hunting, driving, whatever you can both agree on that you both will enjoy.*

Things to Remember

It is good and fitting for one to eat and drink, and to enjoy the good of all his labor in which he toils under the sun all the days of his life which God gives him; for it is his heritage.

ECCLESIASTES 5:18 NKJV

Jesus said, "I have come that they may have life, and that they may have it more abundantly."

JOHN 10:10 NKJV

When you win, we plan to raise the roof and lead the parade with our banners. May all your wishes come true!

PSALM 20:5 THE MESSAGE

Celebrate GOD. Sing together—everyone! All you honest hearts, raise the roof!

PSALM 32:11 THE MESSAGE

You'll welcome us with open arms when we run for cover to you. Let the party last all night! Stand guard over our celebration. You are famous, God, for welcoming God-seekers, for decking us out in delight.

PSALM 5:11–12 THE MESSAGE

A good and wholesome thing is a little harmless fun in this world; it tones a body up and keeps him human and prevents him from souring.

—MARK TWAIN

Whence comes this idea that if what we are doing is fun, it can't be God's will: The God who made giraffes, a baby's fingernails, a puppy's tail, a crook necked squash, the bobwhite's call, and a young girl's giggle, has a sense of humor. Make no mistake about that.

—CATHERINE MARSHALL

Checklist for Life for teens

The art of contentment is the recognition that the most satisfying and the most dependably refreshing experiences of life lie not in great things but in little.

> —Edgar Andrew Collard

I know the thoughts that I think toward you, says the LORD, thoughts of peace and not of evil, to give you a future and a hope.

> —Jeremiah 29:11 NKJV

Choosing Friends

Do not be deceived: "Evil company corrupts good habits."
—1 Corinthians 15:33 NKJV

Your choice of friends has greater significance than simply the pleasures of the day. Have you ever wondered why you click with some people and not with others? Sure, you probably have the same interests and look at life in pretty much the same way, but there's more to it than that when it comes to those you call your best friends. There's a connection, something you can't really define. You just click.

That connection, even if you don't talk about it much, is probably based on the values you share. You don't have to sit around all day talking about values to know deep down where your friend stands on important things like honesty and loyalty and trust—the glue that holds your relationship together. When you choose your friends based on positive values, you are living out a principle that is repeated throughout the Bible: You need to choose your friends and companions carefully, since your relationships will in large part determine whether you stay the course of faith.

The Old Testament books of 1 and 2 Samuel offer up one of the most beautiful examples of friendship in the story of David, the shepherd boy who killed Goliath and eventually became king, and Jonathan, David's brother-in-law and a son of King Saul. These two clicked immediately, and their friendship even survived Saul's attempts to kill David, who had become his archrival for the hearts and allegiance of the people. Jonathan saved David's life by helping him escape Saul's wrath; when Philistine soldiers killed Jonathan, David poured out his grief in a passage called the Song of the Bow (2 Samuel 1:19–27). In it, David placed a higher value on his friendship with Jonathan than on his romantic relationships with women.

The kind of friendship David and Jonathan had is possible today, but it requires a love-based commitment that cannot be shaken by changing circumstances. You can start to develop such a friendship by strengthening your relationships with trustworthy and mature friends who encourage you in your walk with the Lord. Those are the kinds of friends who respect your faith, accept you unconditionally, and motivate you to become a better person than you ever thought you could be.

Place a high priority on maintaining your close friendships; be the one who reaches out and encourages and always gives the benefit of the doubt when misunderstandings threaten the relationship. When you go the extra mile for your friends, you prove yourself to be the kind of friend others want to click with.

I Will

Maintain my values, even if my friends trash them.

yes   *no*

Be a positive influence on my friends.

yes   *no*

Remain committed to my friends despite the circumstances.

yes   *no*

Be the kind of friend to others that I would like to have for myself.

yes   *no*

Be the one to reach out and encourage others.

yes   *no*

Go the extra mile for my friends.

yes   *no*

Things to Do

☐ Ask God to show you how you can be a better friend.

☐ Choose a close friend to be a prayer and accountability partner.

☐ Read about the deep friendship between Jonathan and David in 1 Samuel 18–20 and see what you can learn about relationships.

☐ Send an encouraging note or e-mail to a friend who's going through a rough time.

☐ Thank one of your friends for things she's done that helped you.

☐ Make a friendship calendar of specific needs and specific times to be there for your friends.

Things to Remember

The righteous should choose his friends carefully, for the way of the wicked leads them astray.

PROVERBS 12:26 NKJV

Blessed is the man who walks not in the counsel of the ungodly, nor stands in the path of sinners, nor sits in the seat of the scornful.

PSALM 1:1 NKJV

As iron sharpens iron, so people can improve each other.

PROVERBS 27:17 NCV

Ointment and perfume delight the heart, and the sweetness of a man's friend gives delight by hearty counsel.

PROVERBS 27:9 NKJV

The slap of a friend can be trusted to help you, but the kisses of an enemy are nothing but lies.

PROVERBS 27:6 NCV

· ·

Many people will walk in and out of your life, but only true friends will leave footprints in your heart.

ELEANOR ROOSEVELT

Friendship is an honest mirror, but it must be allowed to reflect or its power is lost.

MARY HUNT

Why Me?

The Lord said, "It shall come to pass afterward that I will pour out My Spirit on all flesh; your sons and your daughters shall prophesy, your old men shall dream dreams, your young men shall see visions."

—*Joel 2:28 NKJV*

God put you on earth for a specific reason. Do you wonder what that reason is? You may have a fairly good idea of what kind of work you want to do in the future, but that's a whole different thing. When it comes to your purpose in life—the very reason for your existence—you are talking about something much bigger than any career could ever be. Your purpose is the answer to the question, Why was I born?

This is where things get hairy, because no one else can answer that question for you; you have to discover your unique purpose on your own. A great starting point is the Bible, where you can find some general reasons why you were born. You were made to worship God (Psalm 100); to know Him intimately (Philippians 3:10); to share the good news of why Jesus came to earth (Matthew

28:9); to help people see God because of your good works (Matthew 5:14 and Ephesians 2:10). These and other verses go a long way toward showing you why on earth you are here.

Still, what is that purpose, specific to you, for which you were born? If you've ever seen *It's a Wonderful Life*, you know what purpose is all about, what life in your world would have been like if you had never been born. George Bailey had a few more years behind him than you do, and you probably won't completely understand your purpose for years to come, if ever. You can get an inkling of it, though, by looking at the lives you've touched in the past and the path you're heading toward in the future. If you're involved in church or a youth group, take a good look at the kind of activities or ministries you tend to gravitate toward. Those activities are huge clues to your purpose in the kingdom of God.

The best resource you have for discovering your purpose, of course, is God Himself. He promises that if you seek His will, you will find it. Ask Him to reveal your specific purpose in life. If you keep a journal, be sure to record any impressions you receive after you've prayed. If you've been keeping a journal for a while, go back and read what God has spoken to you in the past. If you still have trouble finding the answers you're seeking, relax. Keep doing what God has you doing. At just the right time, He'll show you His purpose in your life.

I Will

Believe that God created me for a specific
purpose.

yes *no*

Relax and trust God to reveal my purpose at the
right time.

yes *no*

Remember that my main reason for living is to
love God and be in relationship with Him.

yes *no*

Keep doing what God has me doing right now.

yes *no*

Place my future in God's hands.

yes *no*

Pay attention to the aspects of church life that I
enjoy most.

yes *no*

Things to Do

☐ Ask God to reveal how He wants you to serve Him at this point in your
life.

☐ Write a letter to God asking Him why you were born and where you're
heading. (Be sure to write down any answers He gives you!)

☐ Discover more about your purpose by reading Matthew 6:33, Colossians
3:1–17, Hebrews 10:24–25, Hebrews 13:15, Philippians 2:13, 1 Peter 3:15.

☐ Discover your spiritual gift (1 Corinthians 12) using a test provided by
your church or youth group.

☐ Identify what you enjoy most at church or youth group. Find common
threads to help you discover your purpose.

Things to Remember

One thing I do, forgetting those things which are behind and reaching forward to those things which are ahead, I press toward the goal for the prize of the upward call of God in Christ Jesus.

PHILIPPIANS 3:13–14 NKJV

In Him also we have obtained an inheritance, being predestined according to the purpose of Him who works all things according to the counsel of His will, that we who first trusted in Christ should be to the praise of His glory.

EPHESIANS 1:11–12 NKJV

God is at work within you, helping you want to obey him, and then helping you do what he wants.

PHILIPPIANS 2:13 TLB

God planned for us to do good things and to live as he has always wanted us to live. That's why he sent Christ to make us what we are.

EPHESIANS 2:10 CEV

Jesus said, "Let your light so shine before men, that they may see your good works and glorify your Father in heaven."

MATTHEW 5:16 NKJV

• •

The only glory which Jesus ever sought for himself or offered to his disciples was to be caught up into God's redemptive purpose.

GEORGE CAIRD

The Ex Files

We are not crushed and broken. We are perplexed, but we don't give up and quit.

—2 Corinthians 4:8 NLT

There's no getting around it: Breaking up is hard to do. Having your heart broken for the first time—when this whole love thing is still so fresh and new—is especially painful. What's worse, everyone knows. You feel like dying, and it seems the whole world is watching.

At times like that, you'd probably like to buy a heart-repair kit. After a few days, you'd be all better, with a fully mended heart and the vague feeling that something kind of bad happened awhile back. The reality is, however, that you were born with a heart that can't be repaired that easily.

What can you do when your heart is broken? Well, you could give up or just give it time. Or you could live a lie, treating your ex as if your relationship never mattered. But that heart you were born with still has a need for love. The hurt and pain may have rearranged things a bit, but your heart is intact.

You may not believe God can touch you, but He can. When you're suffering a deep emotional pain, He takes your heart and smoothes away the bumps and bruises. You have to first give it to Him, trusting that His hands can prepare your heart to love again. When you do love again, you will know more about love than you ever thought possible.

In the meantime, take special care of yourself. Get the rest you need; stay away from caffeine or anything else that interferes with sleep or contributes to depression. Eliminate junk food, which can cause your blood sugar—and emotions—to plummet. Several times a week, go for a walk. You'll feel better all around.

Be careful what—and who—you listen to. You may need to steer clear of the music you normally listen to and find something that will lift your spirits. Although your friends may have good intentions, they can feed your sadness by putting down your ex or passing along news you don't want to hear. It's good to discuss your feelings with a trusted friend, but choose that friend wisely. Make sure you bare your soul to an encouraging friend who can keep a confidence.

Will you ever forget the first time your heart was broken? No. But the pain will diminish as you allow God to start healing your broken heart.

I Will

Give my heart to God to repair.   _yes_   _no_

Trust God with my heart in the future.   _yes_   _no_

Realize that recovering from a breakup
will take time.   _yes_   _no_

Believe that things will get better.   _yes_   _no_

Be careful to guard my heart.   _yes_   _no_

Be careful with other people's hearts.   _yes_   _no_

Treat anyone I've dated with respect.   _yes_   _no_

Things to Do

☐ Give your heart to God for safekeeping.

☐ Ask God for wisdom before you give your heart away.

☐ Pray that you'll see God's love for you today.

☐ List qualities (like faithfulness) you require in a person before you agree to go out with him or her. Resolve not to compromise on those qualities.

☐ Read Justin Lookadoo's Dateable.

☐ Thank God for His concern for the brokenhearted.

☐ Decide now to always treat an ex with respect.

Things to Remember

My flesh and my heart fail; but God is the strength of my heart and my portion forever.

PSALM 73:26 NKJV

May the God of hope fill you with all joy and peace in believing, that you may abound in hope by the power of the Holy Spirit.

ROMANS 15:13 NKJV

The LORD is near to those who have a broken heart, and saves such as have a contrite spirit.

PSALM 34:18 NKJV

This is my comfort in my misery: Your promise gave me a new life.

PSALM 119:50 GOD'S WORD

The Lord said, "Then shall the virgin rejoice in the dance, and the young men, and the old, together; for I will turn their mourning to joy, will comfort them, and make them rejoice rather than sorrow."

JEREMIAH 31:13 NKJV

Love is like a violin. The music may stop now and then, but the strings remain forever.

JUNE MASTERS BACHER

Do your utmost to guard your heart, for out of it comes life.

WALTER HILTON

A Different Kind of Love

Jesus said, "God so loved the world that He gave His only begotten Son, that whoever believes in Him should not perish but have everlasting life."

—*John 3:16* NKJV

Sacrifice reveals your love. *Sacrifice*. That's a loaded word—loaded, that is, with all kinds of images. And you never know what kind of images people are thinking of when they hear the word. Some people think of sacrifice as a waste: She sacrificed her career just to stay home with all those kids. Others think of it as some kind of loss: He sacrificed his teenage years trying to qualify for the Olympics, and he didn't make the cut. Still others think of dead animals, and there's no need to go there. But what about you? Do you think of sacrifice as a difficult obligation, something you have to give up for God? Or do you approach sacrifice with a joyful heart, thrilled that you have the opportunity to let go of something you value for the sake of a greater purpose?

That's really what sacrifice is, and God the Father gave us the ultimate example of sacrifice when He gave up something He valued—Jesus—for the sake of a greater purpose—your salvation from sin. The image of Jesus suffering on the cross is an indelible one for those who truly understand what His death means in their lives. It was the supreme example of a different kind of love, one that doesn't take but rather gives. It's a love that carries no hint of personal gain. And it's the kind of love God wants you to have for others.

You know your love is sacrificial when you can honestly say you are willing to lay down your life for someone else. But that's difficult for most people to relate to, because most people are never in a situation to sacrifice their lives for someone else. It may be more helpful to think of sacrificial love as a willingness to live for other people by serving them. It's the kind of love that joyfully gives up something of value—like time or money or even physical energy and labor—for the greater purpose of showing the depth of God's love.

What do you value that you are willing to give up for God? Are you willing to sacrifice your time to deliver bags of food to needy families, or your money—beyond your tithe—to support a special mission project, or your energy to pull weeds and mow the lawn for an elderly neighbor? As you sacrificially give, your actions reveal the God of love to those you serve.

I Will

Develop a heart of sacrificial service to others.

yes   no

*Realize the magnitude of what God
sacrificed for me.*

yes   no

*Remember that sacrifice is not an option for one
who truly loves Jesus.*

yes   no

*Change my attitude from one of having to
sacrifice to one of getting to sacrifice.*

yes   no

*Define my love for others by my willingness to
give up things I value for their sake.*

yes   no

Things to Do

☐ *Thank God for sacrificing His Son so you could have eternal life.*

☐ *Think of what it means to offer up a "sacrifice of praise" to God,
then do it.*

☐ *Dedicate a sacrificial amount of time to prayer this week.*

☐ *Volunteer to do something at church that you would rather not do, at a
time you'd rather not do it.*

☐ *Offer to run errands, babysit, or help out a neighbor in some other
way—when it's convenient for the neighbor rather than for you.
Graciously refuse to accept anything in return.*

Things to Remember

We love Him because He first loved us.

1 JOHN 4:19 NKJV

I beseech you therefore, brethren, by the mercies of God, that you present your bodies a living sacrifice, holy, acceptable to God, which is your reasonable service.

ROMANS 12:1 NKJV

This is love: not that we loved God, but that he loved us and sent his Son as an atoning sacrifice for our sins.

1 JOHN 4:10 NIV

Through Jesus we should always bring God a sacrifice of praise, that is, words that acknowledge him. Don't forget to do good things for others and to share what you have with them. These are the kinds of sacrifices that please God.

HEBREWS 13:15–16 GOD'S WORD

Be imitators of God as dear children. And walk in love, as Christ also has loved us and given Himself for us, an offering and a sacrifice to God for a sweet-smelling aroma.

EPHESIANS 5:1–2 NKJV

. . . .

The key to faith is what we are willing to sacrifice to obtain it.

ELDER CLOWARD

There's only one effectively redemptive sacrifice, the sacrifice of self-will to make room for the knowledge of God.

ALDOUS HUXLEY

Power Up

Confess your trespasses to one another, and pray for one another, that you may be healed. The effective, fervent prayer of a righteous man avails much.

—James 5:16 NKJV

Suddenly, your palms are sweaty, your mind's a blank, your mouth won't move, and you can't find your voice. No, you haven't just seen the most beautiful creature on God's green earth—you've just been asked to say the closing prayer at your youth group meeting. Or how about this: You're the only one in the house. No one's expected home for hours. You kneel on the floor, figuring that now you'll be able to pray. But as the words come out, you feel self-conscious. You wonder if anyone is listening—including God!

If that's you, take heart. Lots of Christians talk a big talk about the importance of prayer, but few admit (or seem to remember) how difficult it can be, especially when you haven't had a whole lot of practice. You need some pointers to get you started, and there's no better place to start than the Bible.

Take a look at the Lord's Prayer. You're not expected to use those exact words, though there's nothing wrong with that. Jesus gave you His prayer as a model for your own: acknowledging who God is, desiring His will to be accomplished on earth, asking for basic needs, seeking forgiveness and deliverance, and praising Him. You can't go wrong praying along those lines. As long as you avoid making it personal, this is a good way to pray in public.

You can also try praying the psalms. Many individual psalms were written as prayers to the Lord. Find those that express what's in your heart and pray them back to God. Since some psalms are intensely personal, save this for your private times of prayer. Find other Scriptures you can pray back to God. "Lord, You say in Your Word that where two or three are gathered, You are in their midst, so we believe You are with us now." Or, "Lord, according to Your Word, if I confess my sins, You will be faithful to forgive me and lead me into righteousness." Depending on the Scripture you choose, you can use this method for both public and private prayer.

There's nothing wrong with practicing in private until you're comfortable with public prayer. But never forget this: God is longing to hear you express to Him what's in your heart. Your eloquence is meaningless. What counts is the genuine love and faith behind your words, no matter how simple they may be.

I Will

Trust God to help me overcome my discomfort
with prayer, both public and private.

yes _no_

Give God my fear when I pray publicly and my
self-consciousness when I pray privately.

yes _no_

Realize that prayer is simply a matter of talking
with God.

yes _no_

Pray in my own way, avoiding pompous,
eloquent-sounding words that I don't
normally use.

yes _no_

Understand that the more I pray, the easier
it will get.

yes _no_

Things to Do

☐ Study the Lord's Prayer and use it as a model to create your own
personal variation.

☐ Find a dozen psalms that you can memorize over time and pray back to
God.

☐ Create a special notebook to keep with your Bible for copying verses
that you can later pray back to God.

☐ Write down what you'd like to say to God in prayer. (There—you've
just prayed!)

☐ Read Fuel: Igniting Your Life with Passionate Prayer.

Things to Remember

Be anxious for nothing, but in everything by prayer and supplication, with thanksgiving, let your requests be made known to God.

PHILIPPIANS 4:6 NKJV

The LORD said, "It shall come to pass that before they call, I will answer; and while they are still speaking, I will hear."

ISAIAH 65:24 NKJV

Jesus said, If ye shall ask any thing in my name, I will do it.

JOHN 14:14 KJV

Jesus said, "Whatever things you ask when you pray, believe that you receive them, and you will have them."

MARK 11:24 NKJV

The LORD said, "If My people who are called by My name will humble themselves, and pray and seek My face, and turn from their wicked ways, then I will hear from heaven, and will forgive their sin and heal their land."

2 CHRONICLES 7:14 NKJV

· ·

Prayer is not overcoming God's reluctance; it is laying hold of His highest willingness.

RICHARD CHENEVIX TRENCH

Let prayer be the key of the day and the bolt of the night.

JEAN PAUL RICHTER

Making the Cut

> To give prudence to the simple, to the young man knowledge and discretion.
>
> —*Proverbs 1:4* NKJV

Grades—doesn't it seem as if your life revolves around them? If you're planning to go to college, your high school records are reduced to initialisms like GPA and SAT whose numbers determine which college will admit you and which scholarships you qualify for. Or if you're an "average" student—whatever that means—people don't expect much from you, forgetting that some of the most successful people in the world got straight Cs all through high school and never even went to college.

If grades are the standard by which you gauge your potential to succeed, you're in trouble! Generally, your academic years are the only ones in which your grades will count for anything. Once you get out into the work world, no one will care how many times you made the honor roll or whether you failed geometry—unless, of course, you've been hired as an engineer, architect, math teacher, or the like. Does that mean you shouldn't strive to get good grades? No. You should always do your best and attempt to excel in whatever you do.

What will count in the years to come and in your future career are your character—who you are on the inside—and your ability to apply what you've learned in school to your life and to your work. You may think that the first will determine how well you succeed as a person and the second will determine how well you succeed in your career. But you'd be mistaken. Your character determines both kinds of success.

You can set unrealistic standards for the kind of grades you'd like to get, but you can never set your moral, ethical, and spiritual standards too high. You may be a solid D student when it comes to math but a straight A student when it comes to loving God and treating others with compassion and fairness and placing a high value on integrity. Which set of grades will matter for eternity?

If your parents are pressuring you to get better grades, you need to do your best to meet their expectations by working hard and relying on God to help you. If you're putting excessive, impossible pressure on yourself, stop. Making the academic cut is not worth it—making the eternal cut is. If you're going to put pressure on yourself, be sure it counts for something worthwhile—like living right while you're on earth and spending eternity with God.

I Will

Trust God to help me excel in whatever I do. *yes* ___ *no* ___

Stop thinking of grades as predictors of my chances for success in the future. *yes* ___ *no* ___

Realize that my character will help determine how well I succeed in my career. *yes* ___ *no* ___

Focus on developing high moral, ethical, and spiritual standards. *yes* ___ *no* ___

Let up the pressure on myself to meet unrealistic academic demands. *yes* ___ *no* ___

Things to Do

☐ Ask God to show you which character traits you need to improve and thank Him in advance for the help He'll give you in making those improvements.

☐ Ask God for the strength and power to adhere to the standards you've set for your life.

☐ Read through one of the Gospels and write down everything you learn about Christ's character.

☐ List the ways you can apply what you've learned about Jesus to your own character standard.

☐ Rate your spiritual life by giving yourself grades in subjects like time alone with God, Bible reading and study, prayer, obedience, and so forth. See where there's room for improvement.

Things to Remember

"Who has known the mind of the Lord that he may instruct Him?" But we have the mind of Christ.

1 CORINTHIANS 2:16 NKJV

The soul of a lazy man desires, and has nothing; but the soul of the diligent shall be made rich.

PROVERBS 13:4 NKJV

Be diligent to present yourself approved to God, a worker who does not need to be ashamed, rightly dividing the word of truth.

2 TIMOTHY 2:15 NKJV

Be doers of the word, and not hearers only, deceiving yourselves.

JAMES 1:22 NKJV

Jesus said, "I can guarantee that unless you live a life that has God's approval and do it more faithfully than the scribes and Pharisees, you will never enter the kingdom of heaven."

MATTHEW 5:20 GOD'S WORD

· ·

For us, with the rule of right and wrong given us by Christ, there is nothing for which we have no standard.

LEO TOLSTOY

Ah, but a man's reach should exceed his grasp,
Or what's a heaven for?

ROBERT BROWNING

Moving Mountains

Jesus said, "I say to you, if you have faith as a mustard seed, you will say to this mountain, 'Move from here to there,' and it will move; and nothing will be impossible for you."

—Matthew 17:20 NKJV

Maybe you've heard the tale about the ancient king who placed a boulder in the middle of a road. Everyone took the long way around it, all the while complaining about the king's failure to maintain the highways, until a lowly peasant came along and pushed the boulder out of the way. Where the boulder had been he found a purse filled with gold coins, a gift from the king intended for the person who removed the boulder. The moral of the story? Every obstacle offers the possibility of improving your lot in life.

What about you? Are you like the complainers who take the long way around an obstacle? Or are you like the one person who removed the obstacle and found a better life in its place? Maybe you don't think you have the strength to move the boulders that are blocking your path right now, but you know the One who does. And He once said that if you have even the tiniest measure of faith, you can move mountains. A boulder is nothing to Him!

Genuine faith in God is an overcoming faith. It's a faith that does not make a U-turn when it faces a boulder in the road, nor does it take the long way around. It's a faith that knows how to cut to the chase, because faith in God is an active faith that gets things done. It's the kind of faith that enables an elderly woman to bear a child, breaks down prison doors so the captives can go free, and renders the bite of a venomous snake completely harmless—just three of the many accounts of overcoming faith found in the Bible.

No matter what is standing in your way right now, God is big enough to remove it. And He'll do it, if the way you're traveling is the course He has set you on. If the boulder between you and college is tuition, trust Him to provide the funds at just the right time. Maybe the biggest obstacle in your life is failure to communicate with your parents. Trust God; He invented communication. Can't find a job? God loves work! Trust Him to lead you to the right job.

Are you getting the picture? The way to overcome obstacles is by activating your faith in God. Take whatever measure of faith you have right now and trust God to move the boulder in your life. In its place, you just may find a life-changing treasure.

I Will

Trust God to remove the obstacles in my life.   yes   no

Focus on God, not on the obstacles.   yes   no

Learn to see obstacles as opportunities.   yes   no

Make sure I'm on the right path when I call on
God to move the boulder in my way.   yes   no

Realize that even the smallest amount of faith can
accomplish great results.   yes   no

Be thankful for the opportunities I have to activate
my faith.   yes   no

Things to Do

☐ Read the accounts of overcoming faith mentioned in Genesis 21, Acts 16, and Acts 28.

☐ Identify the biggest obstacle in your life right now. Give it to God and imagine Him rolling it out of your path.

☐ Memorize Matthew 17:20.

☐ Meditate on what it means to activate your faith.

☐ Thank God for giving you the kind of faith that can move mountains.

☐ Write an account of all the obstacles God has removed from your life so far.

Things to Remember

Whatever is born of God overcomes the world. And this is the victory that has overcome the world—our faith.

1 JOHN 5:4 NKJV

Even the youths shall faint and be weary, and the young men shall utterly fall, but those who wait on the LORD shall renew their strength; they shall mount up with wings like eagles, they shall run and not be weary, they shall walk and not faint.

ISAIAH 40:30–31 NKJV

It has become evident to the whole palace guard, and to all the rest, that my chains are in Christ; and most of the brethren in the Lord, having become confident by my chains, are much more bold to speak the word without fear.

PHILIPPIANS 1:13–14 NKJV

In all these things we overwhelmingly conquer through Him who loved us.

ROMANS 8:37 NASB

He did not say, "You shall not be tempted; you shall not be travailed; you shall not be afflicted." But he said, "You shall not be overcome."

SAINT JULIAN OF NORWICH

The Promised Land always lies on the other side of a wilderness.

HAVELOCK ELLIS

Go Figure

My God shall supply all your need according to His riches in glory by Christ Jesus.

—Philippians 4:19 NKJV

It's tough being a teenager and listening to adults talk about how money can't buy happiness and how you need to be frugal and how you shouldn't strive to be wealthy. After all, you've never even had any real money, just pocket change at best.

They don't lay off because they know that they'd be doing you a disservice. Most adults know that if you learn to handle money when you're young, you have a greater shot at handling it well for the rest of your life. That's what you want, isn't it? The things they're advising you to do now will pay off in the future. You've probably heard it all: Tithe religiously. Give freely. Spend cautiously. Save abundantly. Invest carefully. Budget regularly. It's all good advice. But these are just starting points.

What you need to do is develop a healthy attitude toward money. Money can be your servant or your master, and you get to choose which one it will be. Let's say you make the right choice and decree that money will be your servant from now on. Now you're on a roll. Your servant is there to meet your needs and to help finance God's work. Your servant enables you to live a life of contentment and joy and never threatens to usurp God's place in your life.

If you allow money to become the master of your life, watch out! You'll never have enough. You'll waste your life worrying about how much you have and how much you want to have and how to keep it secure. Since you can't serve two masters, there goes your opportunity to serve God. You'll end up buying things, things, and more things to try to restore the joy you once knew in the presence of God. All that stuff will rob you of time and energy, as you dust it, clean it, maintain it, repair it, store it, display it, and move it from house to house for the rest of your life. Pretty depressing prospects for the future, wouldn't you say?

You can handle your money wisely and still have fun with it, as long as you keep it in its position of servitude. Let your money work for you and for God. Be a good steward of your finances today—even if your assets total only $3.52, safely tucked away in a piggy bank.

I Will

Place a high priority on God's work when it comes to spending my money.

    yes   _no_

Avoid financial disaster by drawing on God's wisdom and the advice of others.

    yes   _no_

Allow God to have control over my finances.

    yes   _no_

Make money my servant and not my master.

    yes   _no_

Develop a healthy attitude toward money.

    yes   _no_

Find contentment in life, not in things.

    yes   _no_

Things to Do

- [ ] Officially make God the master of your finances. Ask Him to give you wisdom for the financial decisions you have to make.

- [ ] Look up the word stewardship using an online study Bible and read the corresponding verses.

- [ ] Keep a log of how much money you spend in a week. Don't forget all those coins you feed to vending machines.

- [ ] The following week, try to break your record by spending less.

- [ ] Count up all the money you have right now. Tithe on it, even if your tithe only amounts to thirty-five cents from that piggy bank of yours.

Things to Remember

God is the one who gives seed to the farmer and then bread to eat. In the same way, he will give you many opportunities to do good, and he will produce a great harvest of generosity in you. Yes, you will be enriched so that you can give even more generously. And when we take your gifts to those who need them, they will break out in thanksgiving to God.

2 CORINTHIANS 9:10–11 NLT

A good man leaves an inheritance to his children's children, but the wealth of the sinner is stored up for the righteous.

PROVERBS 13:22 NKJV

In the Parable of the Talents, Jesus said, "Well done, good and faithful servant; you have been faithful over a few things, I will make you ruler over many things. Enter into the joy of your lord."

MATTHEW 25:23 NKJV

The love of money is at the root of all kinds of evil. And some people, craving money, have wandered from the faith and pierced themselves with many sorrows.

1 TIMOTHY 6:10 NLT

• •

When I have any money I get rid of it as quickly as possible, lest it find a way into my heart.

JOHN WESLEY

Money spent on myself may be a millstone about my neck; money spent on others may give me wings like the angels.

ROSWELL DWIGHT HITCHCOCK

Endless Possibilities

I know the thoughts that I think toward you, says the LORD, thoughts of peace and not of evil, to give you a future and a hope.

—Jeremiah 29:11 NKJV

What do you say when the zillionth person asks what your plans are for the future? Maybe you have a specific goal in life, so your plans naturally line up with that goal; you want to be a doctor, so you know you'll be going to medical school. Perhaps you're not sure exactly what you want to do, but you have several ideas in mind, possibly social work or teaching; either one will require a college degree, so you decide to take some basic courses at first until you can refine your goals. If you're joining the family business, well, your path is pretty obvious to everyone.

Or maybe you're like Nick. He developed an elaborate plan for his life, starting with four years of college and then law school, spending each summer on the mission field. Then he'd marry and wait two years before having children. Nick has overhauled his plan three times since high school, and he's now taking courses at a community college while he figures out what to do with his life!

Making plans for the future is tricky business, that's for sure. You can't predict the future, but you can't ignore it either. And then there's the not-so-small matter of God's will to consider. So where do you start? That depends on whether you want to let God lead or you want to go your own way, hiding your crossed fingers behind your back. If you let God lead, all you have to do is follow. If you go your own way, you have to hope and pray that God will bless your plans and bail you out when things go wrong.

When you allow God to set your course, you lay your future before Him and let Him order your steps. Your willingness to follow Him delights the Father so much that He will give you every opportunity to reach your goal. He'll open doors for you that no one else could open—and He'll close those doors that you should not walk through. He'll give you possibilities for your future that you can't even imagine today.

Meanwhile, what answer can you give your questioner that makes sense in the current economic climate and the future job market and all that? Tell the truth: Your divine Dad is helping you plan your future—and no one knows the future like He does.

I Will

Consult God before making any plans for my life.

Relax in the knowledge that God will not steer me
in the wrong direction.

Learn to recognize the signs that indicate I'm on
the right track.

Be thankful that I have help in sorting
out my future.

Be open to whatever God has in store for me.

Remember that only God knows the future.

Things to Do

☐ Ask God what His plans are for your life.

☐ Listen for His answer.

☐ Memorize Jeremiah 29:11.

☐ Set aside a page in your journal where you can write down those things
that God reveals to you about His plan.

☐ Come up with an appropriate answer to give those who ask about your
plans, and be prepared to gently defend your decision to trust God.

☐ Decide what you can do today that fits into God's plan for your life.

Things to Remember

Commit your way to the LORD, trust also in Him, and He shall bring it to pass.

PSALM 37:5 NKJV

Jesus said, "When [the shepherd] brings out his own sheep, he goes before them, and the sheep follow him, for they know his voice."

JOHN 10:4 NKJV

Let them do good, that they be rich in good works, ready to give, willing to share, storing up for themselves a good foundation for the time to come, that they may lay hold on eternal life.

1 TIMOTHY 6:18–19 NKJV

There is laid up for me the crown of righteousness, which the Lord, the righteous Judge, will give to me on that Day, and not to me only but also to all who have loved His appearing.

2 TIMOTHY 4:8 NKJV

Plan for this world as if you expect to live forever; but plan for the hereafter as if you expect to die tomorrow.

IBN GABIROL

Expect the best, plan for the worst, and prepare to be surprised.

DENIS WAITLEY

The Real Thing

As the deer pants for the water brooks, so pants my soul for You, O God.

—*Psalm 42:1 NKJV*

A woman you know considers herself a highly spiritual person. She meditates and chants and does some sort of thing with crystals and believes in the healing power of a rock. Meanwhile, the witch down the block—no, not some mean old crab but a real, live, bona fide witch—claims to have found true spirituality in Wicca. Your whole family is born-again, and that's supposed to make them spiritual. What gives? How can they all believe they're spiritual?

Spirituality involves those things that nurture your spirit. Because you are a spiritual being, you need to "feed" your spirit in order to be spiritually strong, just as you need to feed your body in order to have physical strength. As a Christian, you've no doubt discovered that the only real way to find true spirituality is through reading the Word of God and cultivating an intimate relationship with the Father through Jesus Christ. In fact, genuine spirituality simply means becoming more Christlike by spending time in His presence.

Other people, like the rock-healer and the witch, often recognize their spiritual nature and sense the need to nurture it. Some openly reject Christ and turn to other gods, but many seek fulfillment in a variety of rituals and philosophies and beliefs only because they've never heard about Jesus—or because what they've heard bears little resemblance to the truth. The apostle Paul understood the spiritual nature of those who worshiped other gods and looked for love in all the wrong places. Instead of criticizing them, he appealed to their spirituality and opened their eyes to the reality of the one true God. Society today is a lot like it was in Paul's day, with so many varieties of religious belief. If you want to be an effective witness, you'd do well to follow Paul's example by acknowledging—and respecting—the spiritual need that causes people to seek other gods in the first place.

If you have had a life-changing encounter with Jesus, you know the hunger deep down inside of you that wants more of Him and less of you. You can try to ignore the hunger by filling up with empty activities, but the hunger never disappears. Nurture your spirit by getting closer to God. Immerse yourself in His presence. Seek to be more Christlike. Fill your mind and heart with God's Word. Your spiritual strength will witness to those whose hunger has yet to lead them to the real thing—Jesus Christ.

I Will

Trust God to keep me from being deceived by false spirituality.

yes ___ _no_ ___

Nurture my spirit by spending time with God and His Word.

yes ___ _no_ ___

Place a high priority on building up my spiritual strength.

yes ___ _no_ ___

Seek to become more Christlike.

yes ___ _no_ ___

Acknowledge the spirituality in those who do not believe as I do.

yes ___ _no_ ___

Things to Do

☐ Make it your number one goal to become more Christlike. Write it down, date it, and sign it.

☐ Read how Paul appealed to the spirituality of unbelievers in Acts 17:23–27.

☐ List the varieties of belief that you've encountered in your community. Use Paul's example to create a script to lead adherents of those beliefs to Christ.

☐ Come up with a daily "meal plan" for nurturing your spirit (such as a certain number of "helpings" of prayer, Bible verses, and so forth).

☐ Ask God to keep you from trying to satisfy your spiritual hunger with empty activities.

Things to Remember

On the last day, that great day of the feast, Jesus stood and cried out, saying, "If anyone thirsts, let him come to Me and drink. He who believes in Me, as the Scripture has said, out of his heart will flow rivers of living water."

JOHN 7:37–38 NKJV

Jesus said, "'You shall love the Lord your God with all your heart, with all your soul, with all your mind, and with all your strength.' This is the first commandment."

MARK 12:30 NKJV

Jesus said, "The thief does not come except to steal, and to kill, and to destroy. I have come that they may have life, and that they may have it more abundantly."

JOHN 10:10 NKJV

Oh, taste and see that the LORD is good; blessed is the man who trusts in Him.

PSALM 34:8 NKJV

· ·

You are not a human being in search of a spiritual experience. You are a spiritual being immersed in a human experience.

PIERRE TEILHARD DE CHARDIN

When you examine the lives of the most influential people who have ever walked among us, you discover one thread that winds through them all. They have been aligned first with their spiritual nature and only then with their physical selves.

ALBERT EINSTEIN

Checklist for Life *for* Moms

There is no power on earth that can neutralize the
influence of a high, simple, and useful life.

—*Booker T. Washington*

Give 'Em a Break

Study to shew thyself approved unto God.

—2 TIMOTHY 2:15 KJV

Researchers and educators agree: Schools are in trouble. Classrooms are overcrowded; programs are underfunded. Shorter school days, outdated materials, and inadequate supplies of textbooks, computers, and other materials make teaching and learning difficult. Yet the greatest problem facing teachers today isn't the growing lack of resources. It's the age-old problem of parental opposition.

Think about it. Every complaint you utter against your child's teacher falls on your kids' receptive ears, sprouting into classroom problems and disrespectful attitudes. After all, how bright could any teacher be who assigns "too much homework" or who's "always picking on my child"? A mom who passes these types of complaints on to her children is also liable to accept as utter truth her child's criticism, "That teacher is always picking on me," or "That teacher just assigns things without telling us how to do them," or, the most common, "I'm flunking because that teacher doesn't know how to teach." God's Word is clear: "Do all things without complaining and disputing" (Philippians 2:14 NKJV). Give teachers a break. Close down the complaint office. Keep your comments to yourself until you can voice them personally in a parent-teacher conference (no children allowed, please).

Then, to foster a better learning environment, work with teachers, not against them. Remember teachers are human, just like you are. They have good days and bad days, just like you do. So make sure your kids are doing their homework, reading their assignments, studying for their tests. Remember, there are always two sides to every story that junior brings home from school. Give teachers a chance to prove that they're not the two-headed monsters your children say they are.

In addition, help your child do better in school by instilling a love of learning. Explore museums and historical sites. Use the Internet to research items of interest from ants to Antarctica. Encourage a love for books and reading. Rest your weary bones, place a small child on your lap, and read aloud every day. Let your budding scholars read aloud to you, too, as you wash dishes or sort laundry. Motivate your kids to read from books on different subjects by different authors. Make sure each child has a library card. Let the treats for good behavior at the doctor's office or grocery store be noncaloric, tooth-healthy books. Reading will help your children learn about language—sentence structure, punctuation, grammar, vocabulary—and open their eyes to the wonders of God's world too.

I Will

Acknowledge that my attitudes about school, homework, and teachers can affect my children's attitudes too.

yes _no_

Rely on God to daily help me criticize less and praise more.

yes _no_

Consider that my children and their teachers will have good days and bad days.

yes _no_

Seek to verify the details of teacher-child disputes before taking action.

yes _no_

Actively look for ways to help my child become a better student.

yes _no_

Things to Do

☐ Become a volunteer at school in the library, lunchroom, playground, or on a school committee.

☐ Pray with children before they study for tests, asking God to help them remember things.

☐ Set aside a daily study time for your children to work on homework together.

☐ Turn off the radio, television, and telephone for serious study during homework time.

☐ Visit your child's classroom during an average school day to watch teacher-student interaction.

☐ Schedule a family forum to ask your kids what worries them about school.

Things to Remember

Let the wise listen and add to their learning, and let the discerning get guidance.

PROVERBS 1:5 NIV

Lazy people want much but get little, but those who work hard will prosper and be satisfied.

PROVERBS 13:4 NLT

Study this Book of the Law continually. Meditate on it day and night so you may be sure to obey all that is written in it. Only then will you succeed.

JOSHUA 1:8 NLT

Truly happy people are those who carefully study God's perfect law that makes people free, and they continue to study it. They do not forget what they heard.

JAMES 1:25 NCV

The good hand of his God was upon him. For Ezra had set his heart to study the law of the LORD and to practice it.

EZRA 7:9–10 NASB

Jesus said, "A student is not better than the teacher, but the student who has been fully trained will be like the teacher."

LUKE 6:40 NCV

If a man empties his purse into his head no one can take it away from him. An investment in knowledge always pays the best interest.

—BENJAMIN FRANKLIN

Every child must be encouraged to get as much education as he has the ability to take. . . . Nothing matters more to the future of our country.

—LYNDON B. JOHNSON

Encouragement

A Powerful Motivator

Encourage one another and build each other up.

—1 Thessalonians 5:11 NIV

Picture a crisp autumn evening with two football teams benched on either side of a school gridiron. What would happen to those teams if the stadium stayed empty during their game? They probably wouldn't play very well, would they? They would lack enthusiasm, focus, and energy. The encouragement from cheerleaders, band members, and fans stirs athletes to play their best, because encouragement is a powerful motivator.

You know that from personal experience. When you're tired and grumpy, it's easy to feel discouraged and pessimistic. Yet if someone smiles at you, says a kind word, or offers you a pat on the back, you find yourself bathed in courage with a hope that will get you through the day. Even without those physical cues, moms can find daily encouragement in God's Word. By drawing near to God "with a sincere heart and a sure faith" (Hebrews 10:22 NCV), you can find yourself climbing out from under piles of dirty dishes and laundry with a renewed optimism and cheerful outlook. Spending time in God's presence is a sure way for moms to find encouragement.

Encouragement is contagious too. When you're feeling chipper, you smile more at others. When you feel confident, you stand taller and treat others with respect. When you are encouraged, you are more apt to think about others and help them "show love and do good deeds" (Hebrews 10:24 NCV).

No one needs encouragement more than your kids. Children face challenges every day, just like adults do. So tell your children often what they are doing right. Offer more praise than criticism. If they need correction for inappropriate behavior, remember to add your encouragement too, assuring them you know they will do better next time. Be specific and creative in your encouragement.

Whether tots or teens, encouraging your kids in their activities, projects, or in ways they use their own unique talents will build long-term results of good behavior and confidence. Reminding children that they are valuable to God, that God has a significant role for them to play in His kingdom and plan will encourage them in their spiritual lives too, and give them the strength they need to stay true to their faith.

Encouragement *is* a powerful motivator. Just as encouragement energizes athletes to move down the field to scoring position, so the affirmation and sincere words of praise you give your kids will give them the direction, focus, and energy they need for a good self-image and for passing along encouragement to others too.

I Will

Spend time with God to find the encouragement
I need.

      yes _____   *no* _____

Find encouragement knowing that I am valuable
to God and His kingdom.

      yes _____   *no* _____

Remind myself that receiving encouragement makes
me a better encourager too.

      yes _____   *no* _____

Remember that encouragement brings direction,
focus, and energy to my days.

      yes _____   *no* _____

Seek to make sharing encouragement a daily habit.

      yes _____   *no* _____

Picture myself as my children's cheerleader,
encouraging them to the goal of a godly life.

      yes _____   *no* _____

Things to Do

☐ *Read Mark 6:45–51 with your kids. Discuss how Jesus encouraged His disciples.*

☐ *List the gifts God has given your children. Find new ways to encourage their use.*

☐ *Write a letter to each child expressing praise for something he or she does well.*

☐ *Pray together for God to show your kids ways to encourage others at school.*

☐ *Schedule time with your children to encourage them in a new activity, project, or talent.*

☐ *Play an encouragement game. See which child gives the most compliments before the day's over.*

Things to Remember

I know the thoughts that I think toward you, says the LORD, thoughts of peace and not of evil, to give you a future and a hope.

JEREMIAH 29:11 NKJV

May our Lord Jesus Christ himself and God our Father encourage you and strengthen you in every good thing you do and say.

2 THESSALONIANS 2:16 NCV

Now may the God who gives perseverance and encouragement grant you to be of the same mind with one another according to Christ Jesus.

ROMANS 15:5 NASB

God loved us, and through his grace he gave us a good hope and encouragement that continues forever.

2 THESSALONIANS 2:17 NCV

The LORD is my strength and song, and He has become my salvation; He is my God, and I will praise Him.

EXODUS 15:2 NKJV

When I fall, I will arise; when I sit in darkness, the LORD will be a light to me.

MICAH 7:8 NKJV

Correction does much, but encouragement does more. Encouragement after censure is as the sun after a shower.
—JOHANN WOLFGANG VON GOETHE

Encouragement is one of God's most joyous art forms. . . . Some people combine a helping hand with a word of praise and produce a grateful heart.
—SUSAN LENZKES

Hurtful Hearsay

Gossip separates the best of friends.

—Proverbs 16:28 NLT

Hearsay. Chitchat. Scuttlebutt. Tattling. Rumors. Call it what you will, but whenever one person talks to a second person about a third person, you've got gossip. Gossip fills the magazine racks at supermarkets, permeates the airwaves during political campaigns, and floods phone lines all day long. But God doesn't like gossip. God's Word says that He hates "a witness who lies, and someone who starts arguments among families" (Proverbs 6:19 NCV). These traits are the pieces of gossip, and these are the things that anger God.

It's a hard task, but moms and kids can make their homes gossip free. Start by refusing to say anything bad or embarrassing about family members or friends. One grandmother confided to a roomful of new moms that she had promised God when she was a young bride to never say anything negative about her husband to anyone else, even her kids. Such comments would have undermined her kids' respect for their father.

Another mom admitted she often slipped into gossip without meaning to, but had asked God to help her say only good things about her friends, family, or neighbors. If you do hear negative gossip, God's Word suggests you can change its outcome. Whenever you hear something negative about someone else, counter that information immediately with something good.

Another way to stop gossip is to keep it from being repeated, for "where there is no talebearer, the strife ceaseth" (Proverbs 26:20 KJV). This is a tough lesson for kids to learn. What mom hasn't had a child come and tattle about the actions of another one. If gossip is one person talking to a second person about a third person, any child who comes to you tattling about another sibling is opening the door to gossip. While the other child's deeds *might* require parental intervention, experienced moms stop a tattler in mid-sentence, refusing the talebearer an opportunity to speak until all parties are together in the same room. In this way all sides of a problem come to light, including who or what started it, why it's continuing, and whether or not it's dangerous, destructive, or expensive. By wrapping the problem's information with prayer, a mom can more easily find the wisdom of Solomon and a workable solution to the problem.

So leave the hurtful hearsay, chitchat, scuttlebutt, tattling, and rumors to sleazy magazines and faceless politicians. Words can hurt. But words can heal and build up too, especially when you refuse to start, pass along, or partake in gossip.

I Will

Keep in mind that words have the power to hurt or heal.

yes   *no*

Understand that God is displeased with gossip.

yes   *no*

Be sensitive to the ways that my gossiping can hurt others.

yes   *no*

Realize that listening to gossip is as wrong as passing it on.

yes   *no*

Actively look for ways to turn negative gossip around into something good.

yes   *no*

Ask God to help me make my home and family gossip free.

yes   *no*

Things to Do

☐ *Remember the times someone has gossiped about you. Ask God to help you forgive and forget.*

☐ *Devise a response your kids can use when someone gossips: change the subject, leave the room, and so on.*

☐ *Compose and sign a family contract stating your intent to refuse to listen to gossip.*

☐ *Require tattlers to try and solve problems with siblings before coming to you.*

☐ *Ask your kids to share their experiences with gossip. Gain their commitment to stop gossiping.*

☐ *Journal your thoughts on the ways gossip has adversely affected your family or friends.*

Things to Remember

When you run out of wood, the fire goes out; when the gossip ends, the quarrel dies down.

PROVERBS 26:20 THE MESSAGE

Whoever goes around as a gossip tells secrets. Do not associate with a person whose mouth is always open.

PROVERBS 20:19 GOD'S WORD

Whoever forgives someone's sin makes a friend, but gossiping about the sin breaks up friendships.

PROVERBS 17:9 NCV

Those who are careful about what they say keep themselves out of trouble.

PROVERBS 21:23 NCV

There is one who speaks like the piercings of a sword, but the tongue of the wise promotes health.

PROVERBS 12:18 NKJV

Let everything you say be good and helpful, so that your words will be an encouragement to those who hear them.

EPHESIANS 4:29 NLT

He who hunts for flowers will find flowers; and he who loves weeds will find weeds.

—HENRY WARD BEECHER

I have no regard for truth, no respect for justice. . . . My victims are as numerous as the sands of the sea. . . . I never forget and seldom forgive. My name is Gossip.

—MORGAN BLAKE

Self-Esteem

God's Flowers

We are His workmanship, created in Christ Jesus for good works.
—Ephesians 2:10 KJV

A springtime flowerbed is a beautiful sight. Tulips intermingle their own unique shape and fragrance with hyacinths, daffodils, and crocuses. These springtime flowers need a good root system, too, to support their beautiful blooms. Gardeners make sure each bulb receives sufficient sunlight, water, and good soil to nourish the roots and help the flower blossom beautifully.

Your children are a lot like flowers too—the beautiful blooms in God's garden. You are His gardener, providing the sunlight of love, the water of acceptance, and the good soil of instruction to help God's flowers bloom. Like flowers, your kids have a root system too—their self-esteem. Though kids may have different personalities or limitations, every child needs a nourished self-esteem to become the best bloom in God's garden that he or she can be. You can help your kids achieve a strong, secure sense of self by helping them discover their talents and abilities, treating them with respect and courtesy, and reassuring them that being different from others is okay. Differences merely make each child unique, just as God intended him or her to be.

Your words affect your child's self-esteem too. The Israelites took this idea to heart when they named their children. Every Jewish name had a meaning—*Emmanuel* meant "God is with us," and *Barnabas* meant "son of encouragement," for instance. When an Israelite mom called her kids in for supper, she was actually reminding herself and her kids what she wanted those kids to be—the grace of God (*Jesse*), the gift of God (*Matthew*), a princess (*Sarah*). In like fashion, whatever you want your children to be—trustworthy, successful, honest, loving—praise your kids for becoming these things. Call to their attention their successes, praise their honesty, thank them for fulfilling a promise, reward their love with more of yours. Give your kids a nickname that embodies uplifting traits too (smart-stuff, big man, sweet cheeks), instead of labeling them with a negative, though maybe accurate, moniker (needle-nose, four-eyes, slowpoke).

Remember that belittling a child or punishing him in public can tear down a child's self-image. If kids need to be corrected, help them save face by disciplining them in private. Soften your correction with compliments before and after it, always noting that the actions are the "bad" thing, not the child. To further strengthen a child's self-esteem, verbalize at least one affirming statement to each child each day. Your kids will blossom beautifully if you actively care for their root system of self-esteem.

I Will

Accept my kids and myself just as we are, as
beautiful flowers in God's garden.   _____ yes   _____ no

Understand that each child will have different
self-esteem needs.   _____ yes   _____ no

Realize that I can help my child build a secure,
solid sense of self-esteem.   _____ yes   _____ no

Remember that harmful words can tear apart an
individual's sense of self-worth.   _____ yes   _____ no

Recognize the value of positive reinforcement
to my child's self-esteem.   _____ yes   _____ no

Determine to treat my children with courtesy and
respect to build their self-esteem.   _____ yes   _____ no

Things to Do

☐ *Research the meaning of your child's name to find the self-esteem message hidden within it.*

☐ *Draw self-portraits with your kids to highlight any self-esteem problems you may need to resolve.*

☐ *Write thank-you notes to people who have boosted your child's self-esteem in some way.*

☐ *Read Charles Boyd's Different Children, Different Needs to match different personality types and self-esteem needs.*

☐ *With your kids, write a self-esteem rap that states one or two positive traits about each other.*

Things to Remember

God is with you; the mighty One will save you. He will rejoice over you. You will rest in his love; he will sing and be joyful about you.

ZEPHANIAH 3:17 NCV

You made [human beings] a little lower than the angels and crowned them with glory and honor. You put them in charge of everything you made.

PSALM 8:5–6 NCV

I will praise You, for I am fearfully and wonderfully made; marvelous are Your works, and that my soul knows very well.

PSALM 139:14 NKJV

Whoever is a believer in Christ is a new creation. The old way of living has disappeared. A new way of living has come into existence.

2 CORINTHIANS 5:17 GOD'S WORD

Put on the new self, which in the likeness of God has been created in righteousness and holiness of the truth.

EPHESIANS 4:24 NASB

Jesus said, "Look at the birds of the air, for they neither sow nor reap nor gather into barns; yet your heavenly Father feeds them. Are you not of more value than they?"

MATTHEW 6:26 NKJV

If you really do put a small value upon yourself, rest assured that the world will not raise your price.

—AUTHOR UNKNOWN

An important part of raising a child is to literally raise their self-worth, their sights, and their faith. That kind of raising is the product of praising.

—AUTHOR UNKNOWN

Sex and Intimacy

We Need to Talk

Make no provision for the flesh, to fulfill its lusts.
—ROMANS 13:14 NKJV

It looked like a typical group of children waiting for the school bus. Then one of the girls turned in profile, displaying the distended abdomen of pregnancy. The sight broke one mother's heart. She began to pray for the child who would soon give birth to another. That evening she said to her children, "We need to talk."

We live in a sex-saturated culture. Sexual programming fills our airwaves. Casual conversations are laced with frequent references to sex. Society has trivialized what God's Word considers sacred. Yet your child's basic attitudes toward sexuality need not reflect music lyrics, sex education classes, or lessons learned in the backseat of a Ford. To help your child remain sexually pure until marriage, you and your children need to talk about sex—honestly, openly, and often. Will you have difficulty doing it? Probably. Will there be moments when your child will nail you with tough questions? Count on it. But you are your child's best teacher about sex.

Mothers and daughters share physical similarities that can help you discuss where babies come from. While teaching your daughter how to shave her legs or about menstruation, you can also talk freely about God's commands against sexual promiscuity. Reassure your daughter it's okay to be a virgin, that there's nothing sexy about giving in to outrageous peer pressure.

Mothers and sons can also share meaningful sexual dialogue. While fathers may deal with sexual mechanics, moms can help sons counteract the pressures of peers and hormones by reminding boys that having sex is not a proof of masculinity. Virginity is not only okay for guys, it's the best choice to make. There will only be one first-time for sex, and that first moment should be shared with a spouse. Remind your child that the sex drive is natural and powerful, but it is also controllable and can be beautiful and fulfilling between two life partners.

Recognize that sexual temptations exist, but there are physical, psychological, and spiritually destructive results to sexual experimentation. Knowing that today's sexually active teens face more than fifty different kinds of sexually transmitted diseases can be a sobering thought for you and your children.

One day your child will face the choice between remaining chaste or giving in to sexual experimentation. Take time now to give your children a godly perspective on sexuality so they can make right decisions about sexual intimacy. Begin your conversation saying, "We need to talk." And then talk honestly, openly, and often about sex.

I Will

Remind myself to pray daily for the sexual purity of my children and their friends.

yes _no_

Refrain from showing shock or embarrassment when my child asks me about sex.

yes _no_

Understand that talking honestly about sex can help build trust between me and my children.

yes _no_

Consider that my attitudes about sex and intimacy will affect my child's attitudes too.

yes _no_

Accept that others may consider God's sexual standards unrealistic or overprotective.

yes _no_

Things to Do

☐ _Teach small children that only you or a doctor may touch their private parts._

☐ _Read and discuss Amy Scheuring's_ Sex: More Than a Plumbing Lesson _with your teen._

☐ _Take your teenager with you and volunteer some time at a crisis pregnancy center._

☐ _Share with your child how you learned about sex when you were young._

☐ _To start a sexual dialogue, ask your child's opinion about birth control or sex before marriage._

☐ _Remove sexually explicit media and restrict access to sexual Web sites to promote purity in your home._

☐ _Visit www.truelovewaits.com with your teen. Ask him or her to take a stand for abstinence until marriage._

Things to Remember

Sexual drives are strong, but marriage is strong enough to contain them and provide for a balanced and fulfilling sexual life in a world of sexual disorder.

1 CORINTHIANS 7:2 THE MESSAGE

Therefore a man shall leave his father and mother and be joined to his wife, and they shall become one flesh.

GENESIS 2:24 NKJV

Let the husband render to his wife the affection due her, and likewise also the wife to her husband.

1 CORINTHIANS 7:3 NKJV

Put to death, therefore, whatever belongs to your earthly nature: sexual immorality, impurity, lust, evil desires and greed, which is idolatry.

COLOSSIANS 3:5 NIV

You are not to associate with anyone who claims to be a Christian yet indulges in sexual sin, or is greedy, or worships idols, or is abusive, or a drunkard, or a swindler. Don't even eat with such people.

1 CORINTHIANS 5:11 NLT

Run away from sexual sin. Every other sin people do is outside their bodies, but those who sin sexually sin against their own bodies.

1 CORINTHIANS 6:18 NCV

The expectation we have of being without bodily appetites in a future life is a very good argument against being under their power in the present life.
—MATTHEW HENRY

Replace sensual thoughts with wholesome ones. . . . Scripture memory works wonders, frankly. I find it impossible to simultaneously lust and repeat verses on moral purity.
—CHARLES SWINDOLL

Piano Portraits

*Rejoice in the L*ORD *your God's presence.*
—DEUTERONOMY 12:18 NCV

You may have seen old-fashioned sepia portraits with dour-looking relatives in black crepe, glaring at an unseen photographer. Even the small children are stony faced. Yet some of these family portraits are different. There's a hint that some of those grim-faced relations might have been fun people to be around.

That perception is probably truer than you realize. Generations ago God's Word was the central focus in family life. Though His Word handles heavy-hitting subjects like faith, surrender, and trust, whole passages of Scripture also deal with happiness, laughter, and joy. These sour-faced sepia relations probably knew how to apply God's words to their lives *and* be fun people in the process. That's what God wants from you too. Moms are supposed to model God's character to their children, so sharing God's joy, laughter, and happiness in your home can be a fun part of mothering.

Researchers claim that three minutes of belly laughter exercises tummy muscles as much as a thirty-minute workout on a rowing machine. Since most moms can't find an extra thirty minutes each day (or the rowing machine, for that matter, since it's buried under the laundry), why not find three minutes today to laugh with your kids.

Because kids can spot a manufactured moment in a heartbeat, let the fun happen naturally. If it's cold and snowy—go outside. Make snow angels. Take a spray bottle of colored water with you, so kids can paint their angel or decorate a snowman. On a warm, sunny day be silly and pretend it's winter. Give your kids a shaker full of flour and let them powder everything in sight (the rain will wash it away). Or let the kids wash their bicycles while you wash the car. Use a hose and a bucket so you can have a water fight too. Rainy day fun and laughter is possible by making tents out of blankets, chairs, and tables. Read, nap, or giggle in those makeshift tents. Keep a stock of balloons on hand too. Blow them up, release them, and giggle together as they fly across the room.

You're in charge of making your family's memories, so let them be fun ones. Let God's joy, laughter, and happiness pervade your life and home. Remember, one day you may end up in a portrait atop a piano. Will you be a sepia relation in black crepe or a smiling mom surrounded by laughing kids? The choice is yours.

I Will

Delight in the life God has given me.	yes	no
Model God's character of joy, laughter, and happiness.	yes	no
Let fun happen naturally in my home.	yes	no
Try to set aside a few moments every day to laugh.	yes	no
Remember that I am in charge of my family's memories of fun and laughter.	yes	no
Remind myself that playtime and laughter can be fun ways to become fit.	yes	no
Encourage my kids to lighten up, laugh, and have fun.	yes	no

Things to Do

☐ Make common kitchen objects into weird hats. Parade around the house wearing your fun-derful creations.

☐ Read Job 8:1–21 to see how repentance can lead to laughter.

☐ For fun let children paint themselves and the bathtub with water-based finger paint. Rinse clean when done.

☐ Let your child use your old clothes for dress up. Take photos and laugh together.

☐ If an old appliance is scheduled for the trash, let your kids have fun tearing it apart.

☐ Go online and do some research to learn about the health benefits of laughter.

Things to Remember

Our mouths were filled with laughter, our tongues with songs of joy. Then it was said among the nations, "The LORD has done great things for them."

PSALM 126:2 NIV

Jesus said, "Blessed are you who hunger now, for you shall be filled. Blessed are you who weep now, for you shall laugh."

LUKE 6:21 NKJV

To a person who is good in His sight He has given wisdom and knowledge and joy.

ECCLESIASTES 2:26 NASB

Light is sown like seed for the righteous and gladness for the upright in heart.

PSALM 97:11 NASB

You make the path of life known to me. In your presence there is complete joy.

ACTS 2:28 GOD'S WORD

Go eat your food and enjoy it; drink your wine and be happy, because that is what God wants you to do.

ECCLESIASTES 9:7 NCV

Let laughter reign when it comes. It is oil for the engines that rise to challenges and work miracles.

—DONALD E. DEMARAY

A sense of humor can help you overlook the unattractive, tolerate the unpleasant, cope with the unexpected, and smile through the unbearable.

—MOSE WALDOKS

God's Provision

My Shepherd

The LORD is my shepherd. I have everything I need.

—PSALM 23:1 NCV

Psalm 23 is probably the best-loved passage in God's Word. Small children can find security in this assurance of God's care, and the aged or infirm facing death can find hope and comfort in the promise of God's presence. For Christian moms who spend a lifetime shepherding their children onto right paths, Psalm 23 paints a wonderful picture of a good shepherd who provides for His flock, who guides His lambs and keeps them safe. What an uplifting promise of God's never-ending care.

When David penned this psalm, he wrote from personal experience. He knew the care he gave his sheep mirrored God's provision for him personally. David provided food, water, rest, and safety for his flock just as God provided those things for him. But God's care for the young shepherd boy extended beyond physical needs. Psalm 23 indicates that God also shepherded David spiritually—guiding him to make good choices, assuring him of His presence when David was afraid, loving David beyond all understanding, and promising him a home in heaven.

The blessing of Psalm 23 doesn't end with David. God wants to be your personal shepherd, too, to provide you with more than the physical needs of food, water, rest, safety, and strength. God wants to love you, guide you, be with you, and provide comfort and assurance for your heart, for you are far more important to God than a baaing ewe or fluffy lamb—you are God's child.

As God's child, you're never alone. God is with you. You can talk to Him, depend on Him, ask Him for the strength, wisdom, and guidance you need to mother your kids. Do you lack a job, food, money? God can provide—just ask. Do you need patience, comfort, creativity? God can meet those needs in the blink of an eye—speak up. Do your children need good friends, understanding teachers, new tennis shoes? God can take care of all of those things. God's provision is unlimited.

His Word says He will give you "richly all things to enjoy" (1 Timothy 6:17 NKJV) too, so ask Him. Trust Him. Wait for Him to provide (that's the hardest part for many moms too). God wants to bless you and your children in ways you can't even imagine. Let Him shepherd you with His never-ending care. The lessons you learn from your heavenly shepherd will help you care for and shepherd your children too.

I Will

Tell God my needs and trust Him to provide them.   _yes_   _no_

Teach my children that everything we have comes
from God.   _yes_   _no_

Believe that God wants to bless me.   _yes_   _no_

Rejoice in God's promise of His never-ending care.   _yes_   _no_

Try to be patient when waiting for God to provide for
me and my family.   _yes_   _no_

Remember to thank God for all His blessings.   _yes_   _no_

Look for opportunities to share with others about
the ways God has provided for me.   _yes_   _no_

Things to Do

☐ With your children make an alphabetical list of things God has
provided for you.

☐ Read Exodus 15:22–16:35 with your kids. Discuss how God provided for
His people.

☐ Keep a prayer journal this week of your requested needs and
God's answers.

☐ Draw and cut out sheep. Print Psalm 23:1 on them for your
children to wear.

☐ Ask an older Christian how God has provided for him or her over
the years.

☐ Play the God Provides game. Name things that God will and will
not give you.

Things to Remember

The LORD shall preserve you from all evil; He shall preserve your soul. The LORD shall preserve your going out and your coming in.

PSALM 121:7–8 NKJV

He is our God and we are the people he takes care of and the sheep that he tends.

PSALM 95:7 NCV

It is better to trust in the LORD than to put confidence in man. It is better to trust in the LORD than to put confidence in princes.

PSALM 118:8–9 NKJV

Jesus said, "Ask, and God will give to you. Search, and you will find. Knock, and the door will open for you."

MATTHEW 7:7 NCV

God can give you more blessings than you need. Then you will always have plenty of everything—enough to give to every good work.

2 CORINTHIANS 9:8 NCV

The life of every creature and the breath of all people are in God's hand.

JOB 12:10 NCV

A God wise enough to create me and the world I live in is wise enough to watch out for me.

—PHILIP YANCEY

Our gracious God not only leads us in the way of mercy, but he prepares our path before us, providing for all our wants even before they occur.

—CHARLES SPURGEON

Contentment

Madison Avenue Madness

My share in life has been pleasant; my part has been beautiful.
—Psalm 16:6 NCV

What mom hasn't had to deal with a child who believes the media advertising, "You can't live without this . . ."? Whether it's a pair of shoes, an improved breakfast cereal, or the latest video game, the wants and whines of discontent echo throughout retail store aisles. It seems a Madison Avenue madness has taken over today's kids.

Unfortunately, discontent has haunted people since creation. Discontent drove Eve to eat the forbidden fruit. Discontent made the ancient Israelites complain about God's provision for them in the wilderness. In more recent times, discontent has fueled wars, torn marriages and families apart, and increased national and personal debt loads.

That's a lot of bad news—but here's the good. Contentment is possible. The apostle Paul says so. After being beaten and imprisoned, Paul said, "I have learned to be satisfied with the things I have and with everything that happens" (Philippians 4:11 NCV). The secret to Paul's contentment? A strong focus on God. Paul knew from experience that contentment is not found in people, places, or possessions. True contentment comes from putting God first and everything else second.

Sounds easy, but it's hard to do when you're surrounded by the I-wants. Fads capitalize on a child's need for acceptance by peers. Unfortunately, once a kid acquires the all-important item of the moment, something else is sure to beckon. To spare your wallet and your child from the pressures of unneeded purchases, look at the things you already own. If your possessions (including your kids' things) were destroyed tomorrow, what items would be at the top of your must-replace list? Consider whether you would merely *want* those items replaced or truly *need* them.

Set some shopping rules for your family too. Discuss the expense of being on the cutting edge of fashion. Determine how much stuff is enough and how much stuff is too much. Contrary to a popular bumper sticker, the one who has the most stuff when they die doesn't win anything. They just leave a mess behind for other people to deal with.

So find contentment God's way. Look for Him in every moment, every opportunity, every decision. Stuff the Madison Avenue madness of discontent, and replace it instead with godly contentment, remembering "since we entered the world penniless and will leave it penniless, if we have bread on the table and shoes on our feet, that's enough" (1 Timothy 6:7–8 THE MESSAGE).

I Will

Remember that contentment comes from an inner attitude, not outer assets.

yes _no_

Ask God to help me be content with the things He has given me.

yes _no_

Follow Paul's example and focus more on God than on people, places, and possessions.

yes _no_

Realize how destructive discontent can be to my family and me.

yes _no_

Choose to put God first and everything else second to find true contentment.

yes _no_

Commit to spending more time on people and less money on things.

yes _no_

Things to Do

☐ _List as many blessings as you and your kids can name in three minutes._

☐ _With your kids, volunteer at a neighborhood food pantry and watch your discontent disappear._

☐ _Read Numbers 11. Discuss the Israelites' complaints and God's provision._

☐ _Listen to media advertising for a day. List advertised items that are absolutely necessary for life._

☐ _Make an acrostic from the word_ content. _Let each letter stand for something about God._

☐ _Serve your family rice for breakfast, lunch, and supper. Thank God for your well-stocked pantry._

Things to Remember

Let your conduct be without covetousness; be content with such things as you have.

HEBREWS 13:5 NKJV

Give me neither poverty nor riches, but give me only my daily bread.

PROVERBS 30:8 NIV

I have learned to be satisfied with the things I have and with everything that happens.

PHILIPPIANS 4:11 NCV

Far better to be right and poor than to be wrong and rich.

PROVERBS 16:8 THE MESSAGE

It is better to be poor and respect the LORD than to be wealthy and have much trouble.

PROVERBS 15:16 NCV

Godliness with contentment is great gain. For we brought nothing into this world, and it is certain we can carry nothing out. And having food and clothing, with these we shall be content.

1 TIMOTHY 6:6–8 NKJV

> **True contentment is the power of getting out of any situation all that there is in it.**
>
> —G. K. CHESTERTON

> **When the heart is content to be without the outward blessing, it is as happy as it would be with it, for it is as rest.**
>
> —CHARLES SPURGEON

Me and My Shadow

These commandments that I give you today are to be upon your hearts. Impress them on your children.

—DEUTERONOMY 6:6–7 NIV

Every mom cringes when she hears her child repeat in public some statement she has made in anger or with sarcasm. Young children have a particular knack for this embarrassing habit. Why do kids forget what you tell them to do, but remember the words or actions you'd prefer they forget? A simple reason: the shadow factor.

Your children probably enjoy playing with shadows—wiggling and waggling them . . . stomping on someone else's shadow . . . hiding their shadow in a larger one. Though playing with shadows is merely a game, it's a visual reminder of how your children view you too. Your children will always follow in your shadow, for you are their example. They will imitate your movements, echo your words, and mold their shadows to your larger one by patterning their life choices after your example.

There's no getting around it, your children will imitate you. Genesis 20 and 26 tell the story of Abraham and the shadow he cast for his children. Abraham, fearful that the Philistines might kill him to take his wife, told them, "She is my sister." Years later, Abraham's son Isaac did exactly the same thing, claiming his wife was his sister. Abraham's cowardly lie produced a poor example for his son to follow. Though Abraham undoubtedly *told* Isaac many things about living life, it was Abraham's *example* that Isaac followed when the going got tough. Telling your children what to do is important, but teaching them by example is vital.

Casting a good shadow is hard, so God's Word offers some suggestions. To set a good example for your children, start by loving God above everything else. Try to please Him in everything you do. Your children imitate you because they love you and want to be like you. The same principle applies to your relationship with God. If you truly love Him, you'll read His Word; you'll follow His commands. Your children will see you "abide under the shadow of the Almighty" (Psalm 91:1 KJV); they'll want God's shadow to cover them too.

Don't forget the apostle Paul's words: "Follow my example, as I follow the example of Christ" (1 Corinthians 11:1 NIV). When it comes to mothering your children, you need to find a mom or grandmom who casts a godly shadow. Follow her example. Christian radio shows and parenting books may serve as your examples too. Your children *will* imitate you, so cast a shadow for them of a godly mom, following others who "follow the example of Christ."

I Will

Love God and follow His example in every area of
my life.   _____ yes   _____ no

Begin each day by committing my family into
God's hands.   _____ yes   _____ no

Relax and stop trying to be perfect.   _____ yes   _____ no

Ask God to help me cast a godly shadow.   _____ yes   _____ no

Trust God to change wrong attitudes to right ones.   _____ yes   _____ no

Fill my mind and heart with God's truths.   _____ yes   _____ no

Enjoy motherhood because I know God is in charge.   _____ yes   _____ no

Things to Do

☐ Read Deuteronomy 6:1–7 to find out what God expects of families.

☐ List the character traits you want your children to see modeled
in your life.

☐ Play with your child's shadow on a sunny day, remembering God's
shadow on your life.

☐ Print BE LIKE GOD TODAY on a card and put it on your mirror.

☐ Read the Bible every day this week. Start with the book of Matthew.

☐ Find a godly mom whose advice you can implement and whose
example you can follow.

☐ Discard ungodly influences in your home (magazines, videos, games).

Things to Remember

Jesus said, "I have given you an example, that you should do as I have done to you."

JOHN 13:15 NKJV

Be imitators of God, therefore, as dearly loved children and live a life of love, just as Christ loved us.

EPHESIANS 5:1 NIV

In every way be an example by doing good deeds. When you teach, do it with honesty and seriousness. Speak the truth so that you cannot be criticized.

TITUS 2:7–8 NCV

I will be careful to lead a blameless life—when will you come to me? I will walk in my house with blameless heart.

PSALM 101:2 NIV

All of you should try to follow my example and to copy those who live the way we showed you.

PHILIPPIANS 3:17 NCV

Tell the older women to be reverent in behavior, not to be slanderers or slaves to drink; they are to teach what is good, so that they may encourage the young women.

TITUS 2:3–4 NRSV

Do not let your deeds belie your words, lest when you speak in church someone may say to himself, "Why do you not practice what you preach?"

—SAINT JEROME

The best thing to give to your enemy is forgiveness; to an opponent, tolerance; to a friend, your heart; to your child, a good example.

—ARTHUR JAMES BALFOUR

Sibling Rivalry

Infernal Fraternal Fracases

Avoiding quarrels will bring you honor.

—PROVERBS 20:3 NCV

It's a fact of life. The only way to avoid sibling conflict is to have only one child. Two or more children in any family unlock the potential for sibling squabbles. Your children's ages, personalities, and reasons for fighting, however, should determine how you react to sibling rivalry.

Very young children have difficulty sharing. To prevent fights before they start, let your children set aside three or four special toys that do not have to be shared with anyone else. Put these items aside in a special place. Let each child know that everything else must be shared without a fuss. When fights *do* break out, let young children work out their aggressions by washing a sliding glass or storm door. Give each child a paper towel moistened with glass cleaner. Station them on either side of the door with instructions to clean their side of the glass. Before the glass is clean, the kids might be laughing.

Remember that children fight more often when they're bored, tired, or hungry. Listen to their voices to see if your children are getting aggressive. If boredom's the reason, suggest new activities to distract them from fighting. Send tired children to bed for a nap or to separate chairs to watch a video. Hungry children often fight over food too, so institute a divide-or-choose policy. One child divides the last piece of anything into two servings; the other child has first choice of which serving they want. This two-child process ensures that the divider will keep things more equal.

As your children grow up, tactics for solving sibling fracases change. Children need to learn how to settle disagreements by themselves. Moms may referee by setting limits to fights—no physical abuse allowed—and by clearly communicating that disagreements need to be resolved. One mom uses this reminder: "Either you settle this nicely, or I'll settle it for you. And you won't be happy if I do." Also, declare a neutral zone for all parties—a place where each child can escape the fight. When combatants retreat to this zone, others cannot follow them there—physically or verbally.

Unfortunately, moms can sometimes be the cause of those infernal fights. Spending more time with one child on homework can be perceived as unfair to another. A mom's verbal comparisons of her children can build resentment between siblings. So be fair. Be sensitive. Dealing with sibling rivalry is hard enough. Don't put yourself in the middle of the mix too.

I Will

Place a high value on each member of my family.   *yes* ___   *no* ___

Recognize that sibling fights are a part of life.   *yes* ___   *no* ___

Acknowledge that I can head off sibling conflicts by keeping my kids from getting overtired.   *yes* ___   *no* ___

Consider that my best intentions toward one child may be perceived as unfairness to another.   *yes* ___   *no* ___

Trust God to help me be fair, sensitive, and loving with my kids.   *yes* ___   *no* ___

Accept that squabbling and making up is part of learning to settle disagreements.   *yes* ___   *no* ___

Things to Do

☐ *Read Genesis 13 and discuss how Abram avoided a fight with his nephew Lot.*

☐ *Separate quarreling children to opposite sides of the room. Give each an activity to do.*

☐ *Offer older children an option: Settle your dispute or you'll be given a distasteful chore.*

☐ *Let angry children sing their complaints and concerns at each other.*

☐ *Suggest an alternative to a fight. Try: "Don't fight, and we'll read two stories tonight."*

☐ *To end a fight, require each child to tell the other five nice compliments.*

Things to Remember

The beginning of strife is like letting out water, so abandon the quarrel before it breaks out.

PROVERBS 17:14 NASB

I appeal to you by the authority of the Lord Jesus Christ to stop arguing among yourselves. Let there be real harmony so there won't be divisions in the church.

1 CORINTHIANS 1:10 NLT

Pride only breeds quarrels, but wisdom is found in those who take advice.

PROVERBS 13:10 NIV

You are joined together with peace through the Spirit, so make every effort to continue together in this way.

EPHESIANS 4:3 NCV

Fools quickly show that they are upset, but the wise ignore insults.

PROVERBS 12:16 NCV

Don't let evil get the best of you; get the best of evil by doing good.

ROMANS 12:20 THE MESSAGE

There is no winning or losing in a good conflict, but a breaking through to better understanding of each other.

—CAROLE MAYHALL

When we train ourselves to attack our problems rather than people, we work our way toward healthy resolution without leaving casualties in our wake.

—ELISA MORGAN

Discipline

Plenty Good

This teaching is a light, and the corrections of discipline are the way to life.

—Proverbs 6:23 NIV

Try this experiment. Walk through an average day in your family's life from the pint-size perspective of your youngest child. Look and listen to everything. With those images in mind, you can more carefully consider mothering's greatest challenges—discipline. All children need to know what is expected of them, and every family needs to set boundaries or family rules that define these expectations. Discipline revolves around these defined boundaries; when a line is crossed, action of some kind—discipline, correction, reproof—is required. In fact, God's Word says that "a refusal to correct is a refusal to love; [so] love your children by disciplining them" (Proverbs 13:24 THE MESSAGE).

Yet discipline shouldn't come from an angry heart or heavy hand. Research indicates that the more positive you can be in administering discipline, the less rebellion you'll have when your terrible two matures into a fearsome fourteen. Even three-year-olds can be held accountable for their actions, so try to praise the good and ignore most of the bad, unless it is overtly disobedient or willful. Urge kindness and respect for all family members too. Let positive words frame the orders you give your kids. For example, instead of saying, "You need to get ready for bed," try "If you're in pj's in five minutes, we'll read your favorite book."

However, just as generals give orders to their troops, moms often have to issue orders too. Most of these orders are simple requests—brush your teeth; let the cat out; put your dishes in the sink. But there are times when orders are more important to personal safety—put that knife down; don't run into the street; buckle your seat belt. Whenever you issue such orders, be prepared to immediately enforce them. Give your children a chance to obey by letting them know you will give them to the count of three to carry out your orders. But, if you get to the number three and your child hasn't complied, a restriction of privileges, a stint in the time-out chair, or some such punishment is in order. Refuse to acknowledge any tantrums, but congratulate your kids for prompt obedience, especially if you want good behavior repeated.

Finally, prove your love to your kids with the plenty-good approach to discipline: supply *plenty* of rest for cranky kids, *plenty* of love all the time, and *plenty* of praise for good conduct to ensure *good* attitudes, *good* behavior, and a *good* family atmosphere. That sounds plenty good.

I Will

Understand the importance of setting clear family boundaries.

yes _no_

Acknowledge that loving my kids means disciplining them when necessary.

yes _no_

Make sure the discipline I administer doesn't come with a heavy hand or angry heart.

yes _no_

Urge kindness and respect be shown for all family members to reduce discipline problems.

yes _no_

Remember that my kids can and should be held accountable for their actions.

yes _no_

Look for positive ways to word the simple requests I make of my kids.

yes _no_

Things to Do

☐ _Discuss discipline issues with your child's teacher even if things are going well._

☐ _Devise a family signal—hand clap, whistle, finger snap—to say instant obedience is needed to avoid danger._

☐ _Read 2 Samuel 13. Journal your impressions of David's lack of discipline with his sons._

☐ _Set aside a time-out chair for discipline problems. A child's age can be the time-out time limit._

☐ _Analyze the discipline you give one day this week. List ways to be more positive in the future._

☐ _Make a goodness chart. Give stickers for good behavior, doing chores, brushing teeth._

Things to Remember

Jesus said, "Why do you call Me 'Lord, Lord,' and not do the things which I say?"

LUKE 6:46 NKJV

This is love: that we walk in obedience to his commands. As you have heard from the beginning, his command is that you walk in love.

2 JOHN 1:6 NIV

Happy are those who keep his rules, who try to obey him with their whole heart.

PSALM 119:2 NCV

Jesus said, "Even more blessed are all who hear the word of God and put it into practice."

LUKE 11:28 NLT

Do what God's word says. Don't merely listen to it, or you will fool yourselves.

JAMES 1:22 GOD'S WORD

I thought about my ways, and turned my feet to Your testimonies. I made haste, and did not delay to keep Your commandments.

PSALM 119:59–60 NKJV

A really good parent is a provider, a counselor, an adviser, and when necessary, a disciplinarian.

—AUTHOR UNKNOWN

Psychiatrists tell us that discipline doesn't break a child's spirit half as often as the lack of it breaks a parent's heart.

—AUTHOR UNKNOWN

Ticks and Tocks

So teach us to number our days, that we may gain a heart of wisdom.
—PSALM 90:12 NKJV

An eccentric gentleman once kept a living room full of clocks. Visitors were greeted on the hour by the deafening noise of chirping cuckoos, chiming grandfathers, and bonging mantel clocks. If a visitor stayed overnight, the gentleman would make a circuit of the living room to silence the ticks and tocks. "It gives me great pleasure," the gentleman would say, "to stop time whenever I can."

Unfortunately, time slips by, even if you've stopped the clocks, so moms need to be creative time managers. Get a jump on your day by beginning each morning with God. Fifteen minutes spent in prayer and Bible study will give you the strength, hope, guidance, and creativity every mom needs. Then, set aside a few moments for yourself. You'll look better, feel better, and have a better attitude for dealing with your family if you get some regular exercise. If you don't think you have enough time to spend time with God *and* to exercise too, combine the two. Take a walk with a headset tuned to God's Word. Ride a bike or swim laps as you pray about your family, your children, your hopes and dreams.

To bring balance to the remainder of your day, follow a schedule. It doesn't have to be rigidly marked out to the minute. Block out chunks of time, using the 7:00 a.m. to 10:00 a.m. hours to get people and pets fed, beds and lunches made, laundry and dishes washed, and the house straightened up a bit. Use another 4–5 hour allotment to finish household chores, run errands, and pay bills. Sectioning off your day lets you accomplish chores and incorporate naptimes for little ones too.

In addition, teach your children to manage their time. Announce that you're setting a kitchen timer five minutes before suppertime or bedtime. Your kids will learn to better budget their own time as they realize how much they can (or cannot) accomplish in those few moments. To keep your whole family on schedule, try posting a family calendar. Assign a separate color of highlighter to each family member. Fill the calendar with everyone's schedule information. Make sure your daily schedule incorporates the calendar's information too, so that you don't miss birthday parties, doctor's appointments, or make your teen late for work.

Turning off the clocks won't stop time, so try following God's time management suggestion instead: Make the most of every moment, every day. Managing your time God's way might just yield some *extra* time too. And who couldn't use that?

I Will

Admit that I can always do a better job of managing my time.

yes   *no*

Commit to starting my days with a focus on God.

yes   *no*

Realize that setting aside time for daily exercise will make me a healthier, happier mom.

yes   *no*

Bring balance to my days by following a to-do list or daily schedule.

yes   *no*

Be aware of the time wasters in my life.

yes   *no*

Recognize that I can find spare time if I manage my hours more wisely.

yes   *no*

Things to Do

☐ *Set goals for this week to help manage time. Mark them off when you finish them.*

☐ *Set a timer when cooking supper to help kids understand the passage of time.*

☐ *When planning your schedule, remember to add some fun time to each day.*

☐ *Print SPEND TIME WITH GOD on a picture of a clock. Post this reminder near your bed.*

☐ *Try cluster scheduling: one day for all your shopping, one day for all doctors' appointments, and so on.*

☐ *Teach young kids how to tell time; teach military (twenty-four-hour) time to older kids.*

Things to Remember

LORD, remind me how brief my time on earth will be. Remind me that my days are numbered, and that my life is fleeing away.

PSALM 39:4 NLT

We live in an important time. It is now time for you to wake up from your sleep, because our salvation is nearer now than when we first believed.

ROMANS 13:11 NCV

Do not boast about tomorrow, for you do not know what a day may bring forth.

PROVERBS 27:1 NKJV

Make the most of every opportunity for doing good in these evil days.

EPHESIANS 5:16 NLT

You do not know what will happen tomorrow. For what is your life? It is even a vapor that appears for a little time and then vanishes away.

JAMES 4:14 NKJV

Be wise in the way you act with people who are not believers, making the most of every opportunity.

COLOSSIANS 4:5 NCV

Most time is wasted, not in hours, but in minutes. A bucket with a small hole in the bottom gets just as empty as a bucket that is deliberately kicked over.

—PAUL J. MEYER

God . . . shows us by the wise economy of His providence, how circumspect we ought to be in the management of our time, for He never gives us two moments together.

—FRANÇOIS FÉNELON

Feelings and Emotions

Peek-a-Boo

*The mind set on the flesh is death, but the mind set on the
Spirit is life and peace.*

—ROMANS 8:6 NASB

Babies like to play peek-a-boo. When they close their
eyes, moms disappear; when they open their eyes, moms
return—just like magic. Unfortunately, moms and kids can't
play peek-a-boo with feelings and emotions. You can't just
close your eyes and make those pesky feelings disappear.
Managing emotions takes a lifetime of experience.

Begin by considering how God made you and your
kids. Everyone has feelings and emotions, but different
personalities express those feelings in different ways. Some
kids are extroverts—the ones in your family who make
others smile. Other kids may explode in angry tantrums.
Still others may be congenial pleasers who do what you
ask, but bury their feelings in their busyness. All children,
regardless of personality type, need reassurance that feeling
their feelings is normal. They'll never be able to stop
feeling certain emotions like love or anger, yet they need
to learn that there are good and bad ways to express those
feelings. God's Word gives examples from Jesus' life that

illustrate appropriate ways to express emotions, like Jesus' joy in the presence of children, His sorrow over death, His anger at injustice, and His compassion for others.

Kids feel emotions at all ages too. Infants sense your feelings. If you're happy, they're usually happy. But if you're nervous or fussy—watch out. Little ones will begin to fuss too. Soothe both of your fussy feelings with a nap or change of scenery. Whispering in an ear sometimes works too. If you find yourself constantly saying no to a toddler, the emotion of frustration may be running high. Shift gears and call in reinforcements: a babysitter or spouse to watch the kids while you take a walk. Let children know, too, that their inappropriate expressions of emotions cloud communication: If they whine, you won't listen; if they use foul language, you won't stay in the same room with them.

To find peaceful, godly feelings, concentrate on the good stuff. Arouse empathy in your kids as you talk about and pray for those who have experienced tragedy. Feelings of compassion can grow in your kids' lives when you actively look to ease someone's burden. Feelings of love and acceptance get a boost when hugs, smiles, and words of encouragement flow freely in your home. Encourage your kids to play peek-a-boo with little ones too, because there's an emotion hidden in such play too—the feeling of joy.

I Will

Rely on God to help me help my kids manage their emotions.

yes _no_

Look for my kids' different personalities and ways of expressing their emotions.

yes _no_

Be aware that my children need reassurance that feeling their feelings is normal.

yes _no_

Be thankful for Jesus' example that teaches my children and me appropriate expressions of emotion.

yes _no_

Realize that my kids are sensitive to my emotions and feelings.

yes _no_

Learn to encourage my kids to feel good feelings.

yes _no_

Things to Do

☐ Ask your kids how they would feel if they lived somewhere without food or housing.

☐ Whenever you're afraid, record your feelings in a journal. Note your feelings after fear passes.

☐ Reduce emotional outbursts from toddlers by scheduling your errands to non-nap times.

☐ Surprise your child with happy playtime in the park—before they begin to whine for it.

☐ Make an emotions poster. Find stickers, magazine photos, and newspaper headlines that illustrate different feelings.

☐ Read Psalm 102:1–11 together. Talk about the feelings the psalmist shared with God.

Things to Remember

Search me, O God, and know my heart;
try me and know my anxious thoughts;
and see if there be any hurtful way in me.

PSALM 139:23–24 NASB

Lord, all my desire is before You; and
my sighing is not hidden from You. . . .
Make haste to help me, O Lord, my
salvation!

PSALM 38:9, 22 NKJV

How long shall I take counsel in my
soul, having sorrow in my heart daily?
. . . I have trusted in Your mercy; my
heart shall rejoice in Your salvation.

PSALM 13:2, 5 NKJV

I pour out my complaint before Him; I
declare before Him my trouble. When
my spirit was overwhelmed within me,
then You knew my path.

PSALM 142:2–3 NKJV

Why are you cast down, O my soul? And
why are you disquieted within me?
Hope in God; for I shall yet praise Him,
the help of my countenance.

PSALM 43:5 NKJV

Be transformed by the renewing of your
mind, that you may prove what is that
good and acceptable and perfect will of
God.

ROMANS 12:2 NKJV

The great thing to remember is that, though our feelings come and go, God's love for us does not.

—C. S. LEWIS

Explosions of temper, emotional cyclones, and needless fear and panic over disease or misfortune that seldom materialize, are simply bad habits.

—ELIE METCHNIKOFF

What's Most Important

First seek the counsel of the LORD.

—1 KINGS 22:5 NIV

So much to do; so little time. Is that how you feel as a busy mother? If it's too hard to find some quiet time at home with or without your kids, it may be time for you to prioritize.

Basic priorities are necessary to keep our families running smoothly. To prioritize well look at your life, your activities, your schedule, and your family's needs. Decide what's vitally important, what can be left for another time, and what is truly unnecessary. Life never stands still while you're working through your priorities. Other things will come along that have to be added to your sort list, forcing you to change some priorities and stretch others until you can feel like an acrobat. So begin well. Make sure your priority list places God at the top. Time spent with Him should be your first priority. Then let God and His Word be the yardstick you use to set your other priorities. Choose to put on the priority list only those things that will honor and glorify Him.

Then make some personal choices before trying to prioritize your children and their schedules. If you work outside the home, decide which is most important to you, your job or your home life. How much time and effort will you choose to spend on each? If you are a stay-at-home mom, how much time can you spend just on your children? If you have fifteen minutes to spare, which is more important to you, cleaning the oven or playing a game with your child? Realize that other moms may make different choices based on their own personalities, lifestyles, or economic situations. Their choices may not work for you and vice versa.

Look closely at your children's priorities. They may be skewed heavily toward activities that place unrealistic demands on the family. Their priorities may be pulling them off to church functions, school programs, or civic clubs. While all of these activities are commendable, you may need to restrict your child's involvement in some activities if family life gets too hectic. Trees need pruning in order to grow strong and healthy; so, too, priorities may necessitate some pruning of activities to strengthen family relationships. By helping your children prioritize their school time, free time, and home time, you'll find they'll be more successful in those few, well-chosen activities than if they tried to do everything available to them. Unburden yourself and your children. Prioritize your lives to find what's most important.

I Will

Ask God to show me what is most important
to Him.

yes   no

Evaluate my family's activities.

yes   no

Acknowledge the need to spend more time reading
God's Word with my children.

yes   no

Trust God to be involved with all my family's
activities.

yes   no

Begin every day praying for wisdom in setting
priorities.

yes   no

Realize that my children won't like giving up some
activities.

yes   no

Things to Do

☐ *Plan a special meal to discuss setting family priorities.*

☐ *Work with your children to prioritize their activities, deleting
unimportant things.*

☐ *Read Luke 10:38–42. What can this passage teach you about setting
priorities?*

☐ *Post a family calendar in the kitchen. Write down all activities, places,
and times.*

☐ *Talk with your children about their activities. How is God working
through them?*

☐ *Pray that God will work in all your activities for His honor and glory.*

Things to Remember

Be very careful how you live. Do not live like those who are not wise, but live wisely.

EPHESIANS 5:15 NCV

Be sure that you live in a way that brings honor to the Good News of Christ.

PHILIPPIANS 1:27 NCV

Set your mind on things above, not on things on the earth. For you died, and your life is hidden with Christ in God.

COLOSSIANS 3:2–3 NKJV

Do not turn to the right or the left; Remove your foot from evil.

PROVERBS 4:27 NKJV

Jesus said, "The thing you should want most is God's kingdom and doing what God wants. Then all these other things you need will be given to you."

MATTHEW 6:33 NCV

Jesus answered, "Love the Lord your God with all your heart, all your soul, and all your mind. This is the first and most important command."

MATTHEW 22:37–38 NCV

Well arranged time is the surest mark of a well arranged mind.

—ISAAC PITMAN

Where no plan is laid, where the disposal of time is surrendered merely to the chance of incident, chaos will soon reign.

—VICTOR HUGO

Wisdom

Hot Burners and Sharp Lids

Behold, the fear of the Lord, that is wisdom, and to depart from evil is understanding.

All wise parents want to share their wisdom with their kids. While teenagers may resist stories that teach obvious lessons, most small children listen intently to the nuggets of wisdom you convey. After all, you are the stove maven who warns of the dangers of hot burners. You are the bathtub wizard who knows that soap stings when it gets in your eyes. You are the sharp object expert who advocates caution around knives, scissors, broken glass, and aluminum can lids. You, Mom, are wisdom personified for these insights.

But those wise things aren't really wisdom, are they? They're just everyday knowledge, right? Not really. Many of the things you accept as common knowledge or factual information are actually things you've learned and experienced over the years. When you remember how you got your burned fingers and stinging eyes and try not to injure yourself again in the same way, you are exhibiting *wisdom*—the coupling of good judgment with information, facts, truths, or principles.

Think about some of the older moms you respect or want to be like. They care for their kids and homes with seemingly little effort. If you feel like you're stumbling along in the dark, do something wise. Go to the older moms you respect, and ask them to share their secrets with you. The areas in your life that cause you confusion right now might possibly be areas in which these older moms are more discerning. Their years of experience can teach you what things might sting when your kids are school age, which burners will be hot when jealousy or unfairness surfaces, or how to handle the sharp can lids of two teenagers co-existing under one roof.

Proverbs 4:11–12 also encourages every mom to teach her children wisely and lead them along paths that won't cause confusion, distraction, or stumbling. But to lead a child in wisdom, a mom first has to find wisdom herself. Asking an older mom for advice is a good start, but don't forget to ask the One who is the source of all wisdom too. Whenever you pray and ask God for wisdom and insight, picture yourself as a little child, standing beside your all-wise Father, listening for His voice to guide and direct you. He'll give you His wisdom, so go ahead, and ask for God's common knowledge. He'll gladly keep you away from those hot burners and sharp can lids. After all, that's what wise parents do.

I Will

Be thankful for all of my life experiences, for they can teach me wisdom.

yes _no_

Try to blend knowledge and good judgment to find wisdom in my days.

yes _no_

Expect God to give me the wisdom I seek.

yes _no_

View myself as someone growing in wisdom and insight.

yes _no_

Seek and learn from the insight and wisdom of older moms.

yes _no_

Recognize that I might have wisdom to share with other younger moms too.

yes _no_

Things to Do

☐ _Read one chapter from Proverbs with your kids. Memorize one of the wise sayings._

☐ _List three areas in your life as a mom where you'd like more wisdom._

☐ _Meet with a friend or mentor to discuss ways to improve your mothering insights._

☐ _Join a mom's Bible study group to learn God's wisdom and new mothering skills._

☐ _Copy James 1:5 onto a card and keep it where you can see it often._

☐ _With your kids, look in Proverbs for verses about wisdom. Discuss wisdom's benefits together._

Things to Remember

From a wise mind comes wise speech;
the words of the wise are persuasive.

PROVERBS 16:23 NLT

The mouths of the righteous utter
wisdom, and their tongues speak justice.
The law of their God is in their hearts;
their steps do not slip.

PSALM 37:30–31 NRSV

The tongue of the wise uses knowledge
rightly, but the mouth of fools pours
forth foolishness.

PROVERBS 15:2 NKJV

If any of you needs wisdom, you should
ask God for it. He is generous and
enjoys giving to all people, so he will
give you wisdom.

JAMES 1:5 NCV

I am guiding you in the way of wisdom,
and I am leading you on the right path.
Nothing will hold you back; you will
not be overwhelmed.

PROVERBS 4:11–12 NCV

The wisdom that is from above is first
pure, then peaceable, gentle, willing to
yield, full of mercy and good fruits,
without partiality and without
hypocrisy.

JAMES 3:17 NKJV

**To know is not to
be wise. Many men
know a great deal,
and are all the
greater fools for it.
. . . But to know
how to use
knowledge is to
have wisdom.**

—CHARLES H. SPURGEON

**The road to
wisdom? Well, it's
plain and simple to
express: Err and err
and err again; But
less and less and
less.**

—PIET HEIN

Checklist for Life *for Leaders*

When the solution is simple, God is answering.
        —*Albert Einstein*

Adventure

Fasten Your Seat Belt!

The LORD said, "Have I not commanded you? Be strong and of good courage; do not be afraid, nor be dismayed, for the LORD your God is with you wherever you go."

—JOSHUA 1:9 NKJV

Abraham leading his family into an unfamiliar land, Moses leading the children of Israel into an uncharted wilderness, Lewis and Clark leading a small band of explorers into an unexplored West, Neil Armstrong leading other astronauts onto the surface of the moon. And now you—leading your people forward into territory likely to be fraught with surprises, despite all the planning you've done. You're on an adventure, one that can be an exciting and transforming experience.

Adventures take on as many forms as there are people. God has called each person to the sheer adventure of living, an adventure that is unique to each individual. And leadership—well, that's a doubly challenging experience, because with the added responsibility comes added grace and added opportunity.

Leaders use different images to define the journey they are on. One that might resonate with you is the sport of rally racing, which involves a driver—you—who must rely on a support team to navigate a tricky route and arrive at the finish intact. Drivers are in the "lead" position on the team, but they need their codrivers to keep them on course and a service crew to keep everything running smoothly. Drivers also need the right equipment—for instance, seatbelts, which serve as an appropriate metaphor for those things that keep leaders safe and grounded even as they take risks. Think of the common sense and the wisdom God has given you as a seatbelt that keeps you from flying off the handle or acting without restraint when your organization hits a patch of turbulence. They don't diminish the excitement; in fact, they help insure your safety as the adventure unfolds.

Maybe you're having trouble seeing your role as a leader in terms of an exciting quest. If you've had a "crazy" idea for a project nagging at you, it may be time to stop dismissing it and start working on it. Imagine yourself in your current position—but ten, twenty, or even thirty years younger than you are today. What would you do differently? If your organization has been around for a while, think of it as a "start-up" and you as the entrepreneur who started it, also a good idea for someone who operates a franchise or serves in a leadership capacity under *another* leader.

When you catch the vision of your life as an intentional adventure that God has prepared for you, the ride becomes an exhilarating one. Just remember to be strong and of good courage, because God will be with you wherever you go.

I Will

Realize that God has called me to an adventure and purpose that is uniquely mine.

yes   *no*

Help others catch the vision for the adventure God has placed before us.

yes   *no*

Rely on the common sense and wisdom God has given me to keep me grounded.

yes   *no*

Understand that with added responsibility comes added grace and opportunity.

yes   *no*

Remember that God is with me as I lead my team along the course laid before us.

yes   *no*

Think of my role as leader in terms of an exciting quest.

yes   *no*

Things to Do

☐ Choose an "adventurous" image you can relate to (e.g., pioneer, astronaut) and find a corresponding poster or piece of artwork for your wall.

☐ Choose a metaphor for yourself as a leader—such as rally car driver or explorer—and analyze it in terms of the way you lead your group.

☐ Ask those you lead to in some way depict the team the way they see it, such as verbally using metaphors or visually through a drawing.

☐ Set a timer for ten minutes and in that time write down all the things you would change in your organization if you truly saw your mission as an adventure.

☐ Select an "extreme" project or activity you've been putting off and begin working on it.

Things to Remember

By faith Abraham, when called to go to a place he would later receive as his inheritance, obeyed and went, even though he did not know where he was going.

HEBREWS 11:8 NIV

I am the LORD your God, who upholds your right hand, who says to you, "Do not fear, I will help you."

ISAIAH 41:13 NASB

O Israel, the LORD who created you says: "Do not be afraid, for I have ransomed you. I have called you by name; you are mine."

ISAIAH 43:1 NLT

The LORD said to Joshua, "Never stop reading The Book of the Law he [Moses] gave you. Day and night you must think about what it says. If you obey it completely, you and Israel will be able to take this land."

JOSHUA 1:8 CEV

When Peter saw how strong the wind was, he was afraid and started sinking. "Save me, Lord!" he shouted. Right away, Jesus reached out his hand. He helped Peter up and said, "You surely don't have much faith. Why do you doubt?"

MATTHEW 14:30–31 CEV

It is in the compelling zest of high adventure and of victory, and in creative action, that man finds his supreme joys.

—ANTOINE DE SAINT-EXUPÉRY

The vitality of thought is in adventure. Ideas won't keep. Something must be done about them. When the idea is new, its custodians have fervor, live for it, and if need be, die for it.

—ALFRED NORTH WHITEHEAD

Boldness

Walking on Water

Do not throw away your confidence; it will be richly rewarded.

—HEBREWS 10:35 NIV

The disciples didn't know what to make of the apparition-like image that emerged in the midst of a violent storm on the Sea of Galilee. Believing they were seeing a ghost, they cried out in fear. The image—Jesus—spoke to them, assuring them of who He was and that they had nothing to fear.

Peter alone seemed inclined to believe Him, boldly telling Jesus to prove Himself by commanding him to walk on the water, just as He was doing. Jesus complied, and, full of confidence, Peter did as Jesus commanded. Stepping out of the boat, Peter realized he was walking on the water! But soon enough, the howling wind and raging sea distracted him, and the fear returned. Peter lost his boldness and began to sink. Jesus saved him, but the lesson was clear—Peter lacked the kind of faith it took to see this miracle through to its completion.

Hebrews 10:35 suggests that you will be rewarded as long as you don't do as Peter did and throw away your confidence. Throughout the New Testament in particular, the biblical writers emphasize the boldness and confidence you can have in approaching God and in your own ability to do what He has called you to do.

Leadership requires an authoritative approach to problem solving, decision making, and the everyday challenges that all leaders must face. Each time you act decisively, you build up your confidence, which enables you to act decisively the next time around. Confidence in yourself alone, however, creates the perfect breeding ground for arrogance; confidence in God, and in the abilities He has given you, is the true test of authoritative leadership.

You will have days when you begin to second-guess your decisions and wonder what happened to the boldness you used to feel whenever you were confronted with a particularly difficult challenge. Don't worry—you're still the same person. You may just need to pray a little more and rely on God a little more. Your faltering confidence could serve as a warning sign that you were starting to trust yourself apart from your trust in God.

Remember that you are a representative of God here on earth. Can anything possibly give you more confidence than that? God has entrusted you to be His ambassador to the environment in which you work and live. Let those you lead see you acting with the authority that only a representative of God Himself can command.

I Will

Realize that my confidence, even in myself, must be grounded in my faith in God.

yes _____   *no* _____

Hold fast to the confidence I have.

yes _____   *no* _____

Act decisively.

yes _____   *no* _____

See myself as a representative of God.

yes _____   *no* _____

Be alert to the warning signs that I'm beginning to trust myself apart from God.

yes _____   *no* _____

Let those I lead see that my confidence comes from God.

yes _____   *no* _____

Thank God for giving me the ability to lead with boldness.

yes _____   *no* _____

Things to Do

- [ ] *Read the story of Jesus and Peter walking on the water in Matthew 14.*

- [ ] *Practice giving your next speech or presentation with the boldness of an ambassador of God Himself.*

- [ ] *Rate your performance at the last meeting you conducted in terms of the confidence you exhibited.*

- [ ] *Read a short biography of a leader like Winston Churchill, whose confidence rallied an entire nation that was on the brink of despair.*

- [ ] *The next time the president of the United States gives a televised speech, tape it and analyze his ability to project an authoritative image.*

- [ ] *Use a concordance to look up biblical references to the qualities of boldness and confidence.*

Things to Remember

We can go to God with bold confidence through faith in Christ.

EPHESIANS 3:12 GOD'S WORD

You, mortal man, must not be afraid of them or of anything they say. They will defy and despise you; it will be like living among scorpions. Still, don't be afraid of those rebels or of anything they say.

EZEKIEL 2:6 GNT

The wicked run away when no one is chasing them, but the godly are as bold as lions.

PROVERBS 28:1 NLT

The LORD will be your confidence and will keep your foot from being caught.

PROVERBS 3:26 NASB

Be of good courage, and He shall strengthen your heart, all you who hope in the LORD.

PSALM 31:24 NKJV

In all these things we overwhelmingly conquer through Him who loved us.

ROMANS 8:37 NASB

Boldness in business is the first, second, and third thing.

—H. G. BOHN

When you cannot make up your mind which of two evenly balanced courses of action you should take, choose the bolder.

—WILLIAM JOSEPH SLIM

Initiative

Seize the Day— and the Moment

I'm glad from the inside out, ecstatic; I've pitched my tent in the land of hope.

—ACTS 2:26 THE MESSAGE

Jack felt his initiative flagging after a particularly hard year. Where was his old drive, that get-up-and-go that fueled his leadership on autopilot in days gone by? After work one day, he vented his frustration to a close friend. Was he washed up as a leader? Should he turn over the reins to a younger, more energetic person?

Jack's friend assured him that every leader goes through hills and valleys—those mountaintop highs of peak performance and the lowland sloughs of despondency and discouragement. He also suggested steps Jack could take to recharge his waning battery, such as scheduling time off to allow his body and mind to become refreshed. He recommended Jack reread the biblical story of David, a leader who achieved success against overwhelming odds. Like David, Jack rose to leadership at a young age and faced obstacles that might have thwarted him at every turn. But David persisted because he maintained a sense of destiny and divine purpose in his calling. Finally, by surrounding himself with passionate people—individuals who see the cup perpetually half-full rather than half-empty—Jack would be more likely to recapture some of his own enthusiasm, a precursor to initiative.

In defining *initiative*, Webster's uses words like *energy, aptitude, action,* and *enterprise.* No wonder this quality is so coveted by forward-thinking organizations. At its essence, *initiative* is the crude oil of venturing. Everyday opportunities arrive, but it takes the courage of a leader to strike while those opportunities are still hot.

Jack took his friend's advice to heart and made changes in his schedule that allowed him time to reclaim some of his former drive. Once his mind, spirit, and body were reinvigorated, he experienced clarity of thought, a refueled sense of purpose, and the physical strength to carry the heavy load of leadership.

As you go about the task of leadership today, look for those golden moments that are ripe for the taking. Train your best energies on them, and invest time in developing them into the action steps that will move your organization in the direction of success. Is there a project you've been putting off that needs addressing? A difficult account you've wanted to pursue (but lacked the energy due to a flagging spirit)? Now's the time to reset your focus on the things that really matter in your organization.

Two Latin words that have become cliché in our culture still hold the key for true leaders: *carpe diem,* or "seize the day." Always mixed with a dose of risk, initiative will keep your leadership vital. As you take steps to recharge your own battery, your days and moments will be filled with the vibrant initiative that sets leaders apart from followers.

I Will

Learn to recognize opportunities in all their varying forms.

yes ___ no ___

Ask God to restore my spiritual vigor.

yes ___ no ___

Trust that my leadership instinct is alive and well.

yes ___ no ___

Be open to the possibilities that God has in store for me.

yes ___ no ___

Reflect on the meaning of the phrase *carpe diem*.

yes ___ no ___

Thank God for the leadership gift of an enterprising spirit.

yes ___ no ___

Have an attitude of great expectations.

yes ___ no ___

Things to Do

☐ Write a sentence describing your God-given destiny, as you see it, and post it next to your computer.

☐ Schedule a getaway to recharge your battery.

☐ Do a Web search on leadership initiative, and write down at least three takeaway thoughts.

☐ Seek out the company of visionary, passionate people and network with them at least once a week.

☐ Think of one opportunity that is hot at the moment and list three or four strategies to bring that opportunity to fruition.

☐ Read the Old Testament story of David and notice how many times he took initiative in the face of overwhelming odds.

Things to Remember

Whatever you do, do well, for in death, where you are going, there is no working or planning, or knowing, or understanding.

ECCLESIASTES 9:10 TLB

Commit your way to the LORD; trust in him and he will do this.

PSALM 37:5 NIV

I'm not saying that I have this all together, that I have it made. But I am well on my way, reaching out for Christ, who has so wondrously reached out for me.

PHILIPPIANS 3:12 THE MESSAGE

Then Moses called Bezalel and Aholiab, and every gifted artisan in whose heart the LORD had put wisdom, everyone whose heart was stirred, to come and do the work.

EXODUS 36:2 NKJV

Jesus said, "The seed on good soil stands for those with a noble and good heart, who hear the word, retain it, and by persevering produce a crop."

LUKE 8:15 NIV

To those who by perseverance in doing good seek for glory and honor and immortality, eternal life.

ROMANS 2:7 NASB

Initiative is doing the right thing without being told.

—VICTOR HUGO

Genius is initiative on fire.

—GEORGE HOLBROOK JACKSON

Competition

Being Your Best

Be devoted to one another in brotherly love. Honor one another above yourselves.

—ROMANS 12:10 NIV

When Betty opened a bookshop and café in the restored district of downtown, customers flocked to sample her store's cozy combination of steaming java and front list titles. It was the kind of place where book lovers were encouraged to browse and linger. Every time the bell over the door jingled, Betty happily envisioned a potential sale at the cash register. That all changed the day a huge bookseller chain moved in a few blocks down the street. They had a café too—and thousands more titles than Betty could ever hope to stock. Suddenly, the joy went out of bookselling for her. As she watched her steady stream of customers dwindle to a trickle, her brimming goodwill threatened to turn to bitterness.

Competition. It's a word business owners know like their own middle names—and one they often live in quiet dread of. Yet, ironically, many business leaders have learned to approach competition as a blessing in disguise. The true-grit determination that makes a free enterprise system so effective raises the bar for everyone—rendering products and services in a constant state of improvement. Those in business often find that competition not only keeps them on their toes, it brings out their creative and productive best.

Refusing to be vanquished, Betty decided to play up her strengths—those aspects of indie ownership that a chain would struggle to match, like overwhelming customer service, adding the personal touch to every sale, and making her store a home for the reading community. Over the ensuing months, she and her staff worked hard for their customers and surprised themselves by coming up with creative perks, such as poetry readings, open-mike nights that created a forum for artists and musicians, a staff's-picks recommended reading list, book clubs that linked with local schools for publicity and support, a finish-the-mystery writing contest for aspiring authors, and other programs. When Betty spotted one of the managers from the chain bookstore in her shop one day, she realized he was trolling for ideas—obviously curious about what *she* was doing right. Instead of resenting his presence, she introduced herself, complimenting the man on the success of his store and forming an unlikely friendship in the process.

It's easy to spout a biblical injunction to "honor one another above yourselves" but quite another matter to live it out in the world of business and the leadership world. Yet the resolve to live by high standards still issues a clarion call to anyone whose heart leans toward rightness.

Competition can bring out the best and worst in a leader. Make best behavior the order of your day. You'll never regret it.

I Will

Realize that competitors bring out the best in me. _____yes_____ _____no_____

Put my highest effort into my business or leadership endeavor. _____yes_____ _____no_____

Believe that God intends to work everything out for good as I put Him first in my life. _____yes_____ _____no_____

Be thankful for the chance to compete in the marketplace of ideas or products/services. _____yes_____ _____no_____

Understand that I am more than the bottom line. _____yes_____ _____no_____

Remember that those who strive to be first in the kingdom will end up last. _____yes_____ _____no_____

Things to Do

☐ *Choose someone you view as a rival, and pray for God's blessing on their business.*

☐ *Pray for God's blessing on your own business or leadership endeavor.*

☐ *Look for ways to add value to your products or services.*

☐ *Select one of the quotations on the facing page and tape it to your computer monitor.*

☐ *Consult your staff for ideas on how to be your competitive best as an organization.*

☐ *Think of a time when your organization's performance flagged and how you would act differently now.*

Things to Remember

Everyone who competes for the prize is temperate in all things. Now they do it to obtain a perishable crown, but we for an imperishable crown.

1 CORINTHIANS 9:25 NKJV

Similarly, if anyone competes as an athlete, he does not receive the victor's crown unless he competes according to the rules.

2 TIMOTHY 2:5 NIV

You will understand what is right, just, and fair, and you will know how to find the right course of action every time.

PROVERBS 2:9 NLT

The Rock: His works are perfect, and the way he works is fair and just; A God you can depend upon, no exceptions, a straight-arrow God.

DEUTERONOMY 32:4 THE MESSAGE

Jesus said, "If someone wants to sue you and take your tunic, let him have your cloak as well. If someone forces you to go one mile, go with him two miles."

MATTHEW 5:40–41 NIV

If your enemies are hungry, feed them. If they are thirsty, give them something to drink, and they will be ashamed of what they have done to you.

ROMANS 12:20 NLT

Goodwill is the one and only asset that competition cannot undersell or destroy.

—MARSHALL FIELD

Thank God for competition. When our competitors upset our plans or outdo our designs, they open infinite possibilities of our own work to us.

—GIL ATKINSON

Many Hands, Light Work

Jethro said to Moses, "Both you and these people who are with you will surely wear yourselves out. For this thing is too much for you; you are not able to perform it by yourself."

—Exodus 18:18 NKJV

When Samantha received her long-awaited promotion to manager, she was more than ready to demonstrate her abilities. This was her chance to shine, her opportunity to show what she was made of. In her zeal to make an impression, she hoarded duties for herself, abiding by the motto "If you want something done right, do it yourself." The problem was that there was only so much of herself to go around. One day after lunch, a trusted mentor encouraged her to relinquish her grip on two or three pet projects and trust key people to get the job done. "It'll require trust on your part, but you'll set your people free," the mentor said. Sure enough, when she let go of the reins, those key staffers in turn stepped up to the plate and showed what they were made of. Samantha's workload is a lot more manageable these days.

Samantha discovered that something magical happens when people are expected to shine—and given the freedom to do so.

Offering up your best leadership skills day by day is what

defines you as a leader. It's what makes others want to follow you. That skill set is only complete when it includes a healthy ability to delegate to others.

Almost everyone knows what it's like to work for a leader who doesn't trust in his or her people. The resulting low morale grows so thick it is almost palpable. Contrast that to the organization that spreads enthusiasm and a you-can-do-it attitude down every hall.

Moses staggered under the weight of leading the Israelites who followed him into the wilderness toward the promised land. Like all competent leaders, he was simply trying to do the task assigned to him—in this case, by God. But his father-in-law, Jethro, saw a man in trouble and stepped in with some timely advice. Because Moses was open to Jethro's wisdom, the camp of Israel was divided into manageable groups, each with its own judge, or leader. God did not strip the leadership mantle from Moses—he was still the one ultimately responsible for the people—but the reduced burden allowed him to lead from strength rather than chronic exhaustion.

Entrust appropriate projects to the people you lead, and you all will win.

I Will

Remember that many hands really do make light work.

Be aware that God ordained the principle of delegating authority.

Cultivate trust in others on a daily basis.

Wear my heart—and my expectations—on my sleeve.

Appreciate that delegating authority is not the same thing as passing the buck.

Be thankful for the people God has placed under my leadership.

Keep alert for opportunities to let others shine.

Things to Do

- [ ] *Think of three projects you can delegate to capable people.*

- [ ] *Let go of one pet project this week.*

- [ ] *Create opportunities for your staff to rise to the occasion, and give them positive feedback on their performance.*

- [ ] *Study the story of Moses and Jethro in Exodus 18 for an overview of why delegation is so important.*

- [ ] *Keep a chart of how many times those you lead "shine" this month.*

Things to Remember

Commit your works to the LORD, and your thoughts will be established.

PROVERBS 16:3 NKJV

Plans go wrong for lack of advice; many counselors bring success.

PROVERBS 15:22 NLT

[God] handed out gifts of apostle, prophet, evangelist, and pastor-teacher to train Christians in skilled servant work, working within Christ's body, the church.

EPHESIANS 4:11–12 THE MESSAGE

You shall select out of all the people able men who fear God, men of truth, those who hate dishonest gain; and you shall place these over them as leaders of thousands, of hundreds, of fifties and of tens.

EXODUS 18:21 NASB

Timothy, guard what has been entrusted to your care. Turn away from godless chatter and the opposing ideas of what is falsely called knowledge.

1 TIMOTHY 6:20 NIV

The king said to the servant, "Excellent! You are a good servant. Since I can trust you with small things, I will let you rule over ten of my cities."

LUKE 19:17 NCV

Delegating work works, provided the one delegating works, too.

—ROBERT HALF

Delegating means letting others become the experts and hence the best.

—TIMOTHY FIRNSTAHL

Failure

Your Best Friend

If our heart condemns us, God is greater than our heart, and knows all things.

—1 John 3:20 NKJV

Thomas Edison, Louisa May Alcott, Michael Jordan, Walt Disney, Ludwig von Beethoven, Albert Einstein, Theodore Geisel (better known as Dr. Seuss). What each of those famous and talented people have in common is that at some point in their lives, someone considered them to be a failure. People said Edison and Einstein weren't smart enough; Alcott and Geisel couldn't write; Jordan couldn't play basketball; Beethoven couldn't compose; and Disney lacked imagination. What set these famous "failures" apart—aside from their accomplishments—was their ability to rise above the gloomy predictions and bounce back from their failures stronger than ever.

Throughout his life, Henry Ford, who suffered numerous setbacks including bankruptcies, maintained that failure proved to be the best teacher he ever had. Other leaders have called failure a friend, a springboard or a stepping stone to success, a temporary change in direction—even the fertilizer in which healthy growth can occur. They point to the fear of failure as one of the greatest obstacles to innovation, because a leader afraid to fail is a leader afraid to take the kind of risk necessary for creative change to occur.

Fear of failure paralyzes even those who believe in God's power and His interaction in their lives. The memories of past failures cause them to think that God cannot trust them with greater responsibility, and their ministry stagnates. If that describes you, consider the life of Peter. Brash, impetuous, and cowardly, the disciple who denied that he ever knew Jesus became the post-Resurrection leader of the followers of Christ in Jerusalem. Jesus Himself entrusted the care of His followers into the hands of this first century "failure." God trusted him with greater responsibility than any of his friends would have thought possible back when he was known as just another fisherman.

If you've experienced failure, even one that was highly public and humiliating, admit your mistake and allow God to use it to transform you into the leader He wants you to be. If you're so afraid of failure that you've stopped taking risks and your organization has stopped moving forward, give that fear to God and trust Him to help you make wise decisions to get things moving again. Stop believing those people who predict failure for you—especially if one of those people is you. What matters is what God believes about you, and He has not given up on you. Even better, He never will.

I Will

Openly admit my mistakes.	*yes*	*no*
Learn from my failures.	*yes*	*no*
Trust God to help me bounce back when I fail.	*yes*	*no*
Realize that risking failure is essential to making innovative changes.	*yes*	*no*
Give my fear of failure to God.	*yes*	*no*
Refuse to believe anyone who unjustifiably questions my ability to lead.	*yes*	*no*
Believe God can transform me into the person and the leader He wants me to be.	*yes*	*no*

Things to Do

☐ *Choose a "famous failure," such as Thomas Edison, and read about his or her experiences with failure.*

☐ *Think about a past failure in your life and ask God to show you what He wants you to learn from the experience.*

☐ *Make a list of all the risks you would take in your organization if you had no fear of failure; choose at least one to follow through on.*

☐ *Help a friend or colleague who is plagued by a sense of failure.*

☐ *Read about Peter in the Gospels and Acts, and how God transformed him from a cowardly liar into a fearless leader.*

☐ *Look for contemporary examples of people who have failed and emerged stronger (e.g., Donna Rice, who turned public humiliation into an antipornography ministry).*

Things to Remember

Not one of all the LORD's good promises to the house of Israel failed; every one was fulfilled.

JOSHUA 21:45 NIV

The LORD will make you the head, not the tail. You will always be at the top, never at the bottom, if you faithfully obey the commands of the LORD your God that I am giving you today.

DEUTERONOMY 28:13 GOD'S WORD

A good person will never fail; he will always be remembered.

PSALM 112:6 GNT

Let us try as hard as we can to enter God's rest so that no one will fail by following the example of those who refused to obey.

HEBREWS 4:11 NCV

The LORD said, "I will forgive their wrongdoings, and I will never again remember their sins."

HEBREWS 8:12 NLT

Sin shall not have dominion over you, for you are not under law but under grace.

ROMANS 6:14 NKJV

We must expect to fail . . . but fail in a learning posture, determined not to repeat the mistakes, and to maximize the benefits from what is learned in the process.

—TED W. ENGSTROM

Failure is a detour, not a dead-end street.

—ZIG ZIGLAR

Learning to Multiply

From whom the whole body, joined and knit together by what every joint supplies, according to the effective working by which every part does its share, causes growth of the body for the edifying of itself in love.

—Ephesians 4:16 NKJV

When Wesley bought a small printing company, it was one of the few businesses of its kind in the area. Compared to the competition, the services it offered were extensive, and Wesley was determined to see the company grow. With the zeal of a man on a mission, he devised a strategy for growth that was as radical as it was unrealistic. He ordered state-of-the-art equipment, began remodeling the existing facilities, and got the word out about the new ownership and upgraded services. He was soon able to hire two additional employees.

Meanwhile, Wesley's wife Cynthia tried to remain supportive, but all their assets were now tied up in this new venture, and they were seriously in debt. She attempted to reason with him, asking him to just slow things down a bit. "We have to grow the business," he would always respond. He was so focused on the growth of his own company that he failed to keep abreast of the local business news—including an item in the newspaper indicating that not one but two big office supply stores featuring comprehensive printing services would be coming to the area within the next year. By the time he found out, it was too late to change course. Not surprisingly, when the stores opened, they siphoned off not only many of Wesley's clients but also his most experienced employees. Within another year, his company had gone bankrupt.

Whether you're in business or ministry, it's likely that you've been encouraged to add to the "numbers." In business, that usually means increasing revenue; in ministry, it means drawing more people. And that's generally a good thing; adding to the bottom line or bringing people to Christ often means that you're doing your job and fulfilling your calling. But not all growth is good. "Growth for the sake of growth is the ideology of the cancer cell," Edward Abbey once said. As Wesley discovered, an unhealthy focus on growth can have disastrous consequences.

Examine your motives in setting a goal for the growth you want to achieve. If you're in business, the consequences of an unhealthy focus on growth include financial ruin. In ministry, the consequences are even heavier if the increased numbers fail to represent lives genuinely changed by God. In both cases, people are devalued; if the leadership sees each person—whether customer or convert—as just another number, each person will begin to feel like just another number. That's not healthy, nor is it the way you want your leadership to be perceived. Growth is good, but only if it stems from a healthy motivation.

I Will

Develop a healthy attitude toward growth.   yes _____ no _____

Realize that not all growth is good.   yes _____ no _____

Seek God's guidance before making growth-related
decisions.   yes _____ no _____

Place a higher value on people than on the numbers
they represent.   yes _____ no _____

Be aware of the consequences of an unhealthy focus
on growth.   yes _____ no _____

Take circumstances and others' opinions into
account when planning for growth.   yes _____ no _____

Things to Do

- [ ] *Assess your organization's current approach to growth.*

- [ ] *Create short- and long-range growth plans (or revise existing plans) after you've spent time in prayer about it.*

- [ ] *Start a pro-and-con list relating to growth in your organization (a pro may be "evidence of successful outreach," while a con may be "need larger facilities"). Analyze the results.*

- [ ] *Read the story of the explosive growth of the early church in Acts 2— and consider the task Peter had as the leader of three thousand new converts all at once.*

- [ ] *Look at your group's history of growth and determine what accounted for any spikes in growth.*

- [ ] *Ask your team for ideas on how to make your organization grow in a healthy way.*

Things to Remember

The word of God spread. The number of disciples in Jerusalem increased rapidly, and a large number of priests became obedient to the faith.

ACTS 6:7 NIV

I planted, Apollos watered, but God was causing the growth.

1 CORINTHIANS 3:6 NASB

I plan to be around awhile, companion to you as your growth and joy in this life of trusting God continues.

PHILIPPIANS 1:25 THE MESSAGE

May the LORD, the God of your fathers, increase you a thousand times and bless you as he has promised!

DEUTERONOMY 1:11 NIV

I command you today to love the LORD your God, to walk in his ways, and to keep his commands, decrees and laws; then you will live and increase, and the LORD your God will bless you in the land you are entering to possess.

DEUTERONOMY 30:16 NIV

The LORD said, "I will look on you with favor and make you fruitful and increase your numbers, and I will keep my covenant with you."

LEVITICUS 26:9 NIV

The fatal metaphor of progress, which means leaving things behind us, has utterly obscured the real idea of growth, which means leaving things inside us.

—G. K. CHESTERTON

We grow because we struggle, we learn, and we overcome.

—R. C. ALLEN

Commitment

The Power of Persistence

Jesus said, "But he who endures to the end shall be saved."
—MATTHEW 24:13 NKJV

Janet saw the handwriting on the wall and interpreted it accurately. As president of a small, local chapter of a national association of public speakers, she knew their charter was likely to be rescinded. Membership had fallen off, and their numbers had recently dipped below the minimum that was required to keep the chapter afloat. The members of the group genuinely liked each other and worked well together—and that, she reasoned, may have been part of the problem. They had become insular.

Resolved to keep the chapter alive, Janet began single-handedly recruiting new members—as well as volunteers from among the current membership who would mentor the new people. Furthermore, she began lining up paid speaking engagements for some of the more seasoned members of the chapter, something that fell clearly into the category of over and above the line of duty.

Though Janet worked largely in the background, the results of her efforts were evident, and a grateful membership responded enthusiastically to her commitment to keeping the chapter going. Soon, they began recruiting new members, and the mentoring program accomplished the desired effect of shifting the existing members' focus beyond their tight-knit group. The result? The chapter not only survived but also thrived and within two years became a model for growth and relationship-building for the entire association.

Janet's actions underscored four of the basic qualities of effective, committed leaders: They persevere through the rough times. They do what they want their followers to do. They know when to change course. They are personally invested in the work they do. But there's one more: They know when it's time to quit. That one didn't figure in to Janet's situation, because her team got on board with her. But if they hadn't, and if through prayer and reflection Janet had determined that the group no longer served the purpose for which it was intended, then she would have been in a position to make the difficult decision to let go. Propping up a team that has outlived its purpose is no better than giving up in defeat because you lack the commitment to keep it going.

The strength to persevere through the rough times ultimately comes from God, though your own personal resolve and the support of your team also factor in to the steadfastness of your commitment. Your team is looking to you as its leader to keep them pressing toward their goals even when the challenges seem insurmountable. Once you've determined that those goals are still valid, keep your eyes on them—and on God—and don't think about looking back.

I Will

Remain committed to my personal and organizational mission.

yes _no_

Surround myself with equally committed people.

yes _no_

Realize that commitment from my team does not mean conformity to a rigid set of ideas.

yes _no_

Trust God to strengthen me when fatigue sets in.

yes _no_

Remain joyful despite the obstacles.

yes _no_

Know when to quit.

yes _no_

Be open to Spirit-led changes in the program.

yes _no_

Things to Do

☐ _Read about perseverance in James 1._

☐ _Encourage someone who's having a rough time staying committed._

☐ _Communicate your understanding of commitment to your team._

☐ _Eliminate any activities that you are no longer committed to, if possible._

☐ _Write out your mission statement to refer to when your sense of commitment begins to falter._

☐ _Recommit yourself to your relationship with God, in prayer and on paper._

☐ _Read an inspiring story of someone like cyclist Lance Armstrong who persevered against all odds._

Things to Remember

Since God has so generously let us in on what he is doing, we're not about to throw up our hands and walk off the job just because we run into occasional hard times.

2 CORINTHIANS 4:1 THE MESSAGE

Consider it pure joy, my brothers, whenever you face trials of many kinds, because you know that the testing of your faith develops perseverance. Perseverance must finish its work so that you may be mature and complete, not lacking anything.

JAMES 1:2–4 NIV

So we built the wall, and the entire wall was joined together up to half its height, for the people had a mind to work.

NEHEMIAH 4:6 NKJV

We have become partakers of Christ if we hold the beginning of our confidence steadfast to the end.

HEBREWS 3:14 NKJV

May the God of all grace, who called us to His eternal glory by Christ Jesus, after you have suffered a while, perfect, establish, strengthen, and settle you.

1 PETER 5:10 NKJV

If you don't invest very much, then defeat doesn't hurt very much and winning is not very exciting.

—DICK VERMEIL

We would rather have one man or woman working with us than three merely working for us.

—J. DABNEY DAY

Who's in Control Here?

To knowledge [add] self-control, to self-control perseverance, to perseverance godliness.

—2 PETER 1:6 NKJV

A strong leader is a self-disciplined leader, regardless of the mission or track record of the organization they lead. Can you imagine leaders who demand discipline and line-toeing by their team but eschew the rules themselves? Such leaders foster little respect. Contrast that with leaders who practice self-control day in and day out. Others may watch for them to trip up, but the habit of self-discipline is so ingrained in them that it's become second nature—or, perhaps, their new nature in Christ.

The ability to govern oneself in a right manner is foundational to success in leadership. Self-discipline in leadership can run a large gamut, from avoiding situations that hint at sexual impropriety, to arriving at work on time, to keeping your business ethics accountable to a mentor. Anyone who seeks to lead in a God-honoring way will discover, as the apostle Peter did, that self-discipline begets perseverance, which in turn begets godliness.

In the movie *Master and Commander*, actor Russell Crowe depicts a sea captain who is both respected and well-liked, but

Captain Jack Aubrey is not above disciplining a sailor who shows insubordination to a ranking officer. In a private conversation with the weak-kneed midshipman, he encourages the man to show strong leadership and to follow his own example. Captain Jack consistently puts the needs of his ship— and the larger mission of serving the British empire—before his own needs or preferences, exemplifying self-discipline in action. He knows that any team instinctively respects a leader who sets rules and then follows them himself. The men do indeed respect Captain Jack and even call him "Lucky Jack" for his reputation of bringing the *Surprise* through the worst of storms intact.

Larry felt the temptation to let his eyes wander every day at the office. One of the women in his department wore provocative clothing, despite the corporate dress code and at least two previous warnings. It didn't help that she was attractive. Being the boss, Larry knew he had to set a godly example among the men on his team. Whenever he addressed the woman, he looked her in the eye and treated her as a person, not an object. And though he heard the snickers from the other males, he refused to take part in their coarse jesting behind the woman's back.

Finally, Larry asked the personnel director—a woman—to intervene and give the female employee an ultimatum: either adhere to the company wardrobe of modest dress or be out of a job. When she realized he meant business, the woman changed her mode of dress, and the other men started treating her with more respect. Although he remained behind the scenes throughout the situation, Larry knew he'd taken the high road—and kept his own thoughts and actions clean.

The apostle Paul couldn't emphasize self-control often enough among the early churches he wrote to in his letters. To the Christians in Galatia, he implored, "So I say, live by the Spirit, and you will not gratify the desires of the sinful nature. For the sinful nature desires what is contrary to the Spirit, and the Spirit what is contrary to the sinful nature. . . . The acts of the sinful nature are obvious: sexual immorality, impurity and debauchery; idolatry and witchcraft; hatred, discord, jealousy, fits of rage, selfish ambition, dissensions, factions and envy; drunkenness, orgies, and the like. I warn you, as I did before, that those who like this will not inherit the kingdom of God" (Galatians 5:16–17, 19–21 NIV).

What was fitting for a godly leader in the time of the apostles has not changed with the progression of time. Like the men and women of Paul's day, you live in a culture given to self-indulgence, one that denies few pleasures. But in the midst of this worldly indulgence you stand out like a beacon on a hill, showing a better way for those who want to live moral lives.

Stop and take inventory of your own leadership right now. Have you faced situations in which you could have bent the rules for yourself—and no one would have been the wiser? The temptation to exempt yourself from unpleasant tasks, for whatever reason, is a constant threat to leaders. But if you govern your life, your leadership, and your organization by the Golden Rule book, you will always earn the respect and admiration of those you lead.

I Will

Allow God to reveal areas of my life where I lack self-control.

yes   *no*

Trust God to help me live a life of self-discipline both in private and in front of those I lead.

yes   *no*

Realize that I will make mistakes, but not be afraid to admit those mistakes.

yes   *no*

Determine to practice self-discipline in my leadership role.

yes   *no*

Realize that others look to me as a role model and take that responsibility seriously.

yes   *no*

Things to Do

☐ *Reflect on two or three times when you didn't practice self-discipline. Recast those scenarios with a positive outcome—what you would do differently if you could do them over again.*

☐ *Write out an action plan detailing two or three things you can do daily to stay on the high road of self-discipline.*

☐ *Ask God for the strength to exercise self-discipline when temptations arise.*

☐ *Confide in a mentor about the one area you struggle with most in your leadership.*

☐ *Pinpoint any gray areas of self-control, and have your accountability partner ask you about them weekly.*

☐ *Read the story of Joseph in the Old Testament to see how he handled temptation as a leader (Genesis 39).*

Your Greatest Asset

If any of you lacks wisdom, let him ask of God, who gives to all liberally and without reproach, and it will be given to him.

—JAMES 1:5 NKJV

A young man grows up in a wealthy household, pampered with everything his heart desires. No luxury is too great, for this is the son of a king. Yet, despite all the trappings of wealth and prestige, the young man is taught godly virtues from the time he can crawl. He learns the words of God at his mother's knee, and they sink deep roots into his heart where they will bear fruit one day.

Eventually the young man grows into maturity, and the day comes when he ascends to his father's throne. Unlike other kings, he remembers the teachings of his youth, and he talks with God often. Pleased with the new king's devout heart, God tells him He will give him whatever he desires. The king might ask God for endless monetary success or long life, but instead he asks for wisdom. He asks the Lord's help that he might rule the people with understanding.

Get wisdom? Those aren't words you hear too often these days, but anyone who aspires to godly leadership will seek this treasure. Every day you face choices and situations that test the mettle of your leadership. How you respond in the midst of leadership crises shows your true colors and can mean the difference between success or mediocrity.

Each Sunday night Jeff faced a crowd of youthful faces that betrayed the signs of their time—some eager, some jaded, some cynical, and others alternately defiant or questioning. As a youth pastor, Jeff strived to teach the teenagers in his care how to chart a godly course through a dark world of sex, drugs, and rock 'n' roll. At times the task seemed overwhelming, and he often felt unfit for the job as he shuffled to the parking lot after the meetings.

One night his head pastor took Jeff aside after the youth meeting. Looking him in the eye, he told Jeff what a difference he was making with the kids, how many of them seemed to respond to his nonintimidating leadership, and about the approval of several parents in the congregation. The pastor reminded Jeff of everything he was doing right and gave him some timely counsel. Starting the next week, he suggested, why not appoint two or three teenage group leaders to work with small pockets of their peers in get-real sessions—times of prayer, reading the Bible, and sharing hurts and needs. Jeff would circulate among the groups offering leadership; the kids would get to know each other better and gradually drop their walls of defense.

After three months of get-real sessions, Jeff stopped by the pastor's office one night. He thanked him for being a wise mentor and for investing in his life as a youth leader. Wisdom sets godly leadership apart from the pack.

I Will

Regard wisdom as a priceless treasure, worthy of possessing. _yes_ _no_

Allow myself to grow in wisdom and grace through the years of my leadership. _yes_ _no_

View mistakes as opportunities to grow. _yes_ _no_

Look for ways to impart wisdom to those I lead. _yes_ _no_

Expect God to bless me with the wisdom that I seek. _yes_ _no_

When it comes to wisdom, I will examine my own heart more than I examine the hearts of others. _yes_ _no_

Make the gaining of wisdom a primary goal in life. _yes_ _no_

Things to Do

☐ *Read the book of Proverbs and tally how often it mentions wisdom.*

☐ *Find a proverb that has personal meaning for you, write it down, and post it where you'll see it daily.*

☐ *Think of an area in which you would like to improve, and seek the wisdom of a mentor about it.*

☐ *Look for opportunities to share with others the wisdom you've gained in leadership.*

☐ *Ask God to give you wisdom.*

☐ *Ask your mentor to share a story about how he or she gained wisdom in leadership.*

Things to Remember

You desire honesty from the heart, so you can teach me to be wise in my inmost being.

PSALM 51:6 NLT

Solomon was brilliant. God had blessed him with insight and understanding.

1 KINGS 4:29 CEV

Blessed is the one who finds wisdom. Blessed is the one who gains understanding. Wisdom pays better than silver does. She earns more than gold does.

PROVERBS 3:13–14 NIrV

The fear of the LORD is the beginning of wisdom; all who follow his precepts have good understanding. To him belongs eternal praise.

PSALM 111:10 NIV

So teach us to number our days, that we may present to You a heart of wisdom.

PSALM 90:12 NASB

The life-giving Spirit of GOD will hover over him, the Spirit that brings wisdom and understanding, the Spirit that gives direction and builds strength, the Spirit that instills knowledge and Fear-of-GOD.

ISAIAH 11:2 THE MESSAGE

What is the price of experience? Do men buy it for a song? Or wisdom for a dance in the street? No, it is bought with the price of all the man hath, his house, his wife, his children.

—WILLIAM BLAKE

Time ripens all things; no man is born wise.

—MIGUEL DE CERVANTES

Checklist for Life *for* Graduates

*Facing it, always facing it, that's the way to get through.
Face it.*

> —Joseph Conrad

*You will show me the path of life; in Your presence is
fullness of joy; at Your right hand are pleasures
forevermore.*

> —Psalm 16:11 NKJV

Where Do I Go from Here?

I know that nothing is better for them than to rejoice, and to do good in their lives, and also that every man should eat and drink and enjoy the good of all his labor—it is the gift of God.
—ECCLESIASTES 3:12–13 NKJV

Sheila always knew she wanted to be a doctor. She refined that goal a few times, finally settling on a career in obstetrics. Joel had planned to join the family business after he earned his MBA. Before entering graduate school, he had a change of heart and decided to pursue a career in the air force. Heather watched her two classmates over the years with a twinge of envy. She had lots of interests but no career goals—not when she graduated from high school, not even when she graduated from college with a degree in history.

Three graduates, three very different experiences. Whether you're certain what career you want to pursue or you've already changed your mind once or twice or you have no clear direction, as a graduate you are facing countless questions about your future. Some are practical: Do you have enough money (or will you make enough money) to live on? Some are urgent: Three companies have offered you a job; which one should you take? Some, however, are extremely important but often go unasked: Is this really what God wants for you? Is this your heart's desire, or are you just out to make a lot of money? Will your plans contribute to the good of society?

Make a list of all those practical, urgent, and extremely important concerns that you have. Turn each item into a question to ask God. Write down the answers that you believe He is giving you; take time and don't attempt to rush God. Over the coming days, weeks, and even months, be alert to anything that appears to lead in a certain direction. Pray about everything that seems to point toward a specific future for you.

The Bible assures you that confusion does not come from God (1 Corinthians 14:33). If you're feeling confused about your career choice, ask Him to give you clarity. It's not unusual for graduates to question the path they've chosen for their future. You can trust that as long as you are on right terms with God—that you want to do His will and are willing to obey Him—then He will open every door of opportunity for you. Those doors may lead you to the career you've been preparing for, or they may lead to an entirely different future. You can rest assured that whatever skills and knowledge you have acquired so far will be put to use regardless of the path you pursue.

I Will

Trust God with every aspect of my future.   *yes* _____ *no* _____

Carefully consider the important questions that
apply to my career choice.   *yes* _____ *no* _____

Be confident that God will give me clarity about
my future.   *yes* _____ *no* _____

Be prepared for God to change my direction.   *yes* _____ *no* _____

Recognize the value of all the skills and knowledge
I have acquired so far.   *yes* _____ *no* _____

Give my confusion to God.   *yes* _____ *no* _____

Be willing to obey God, no matter where He
leads me.   *yes* _____ *no* _____

Things to Do

- [ ] *Make a list of all of the concerns you have about your future—practical, urgent, and extremely important.*

- [ ] *Pray over your list and write down the answers God gives you.*

- [ ] *Discuss your concerns with your parents and an instructor, counselor, mentor, or pastor.*

- [ ] *Decide that until God gives you clear direction, you will not dismiss any of your options, such as college, grad school, military, self-employment, traditional job, or the mission field.*

- [ ] *Thank God that you have options to choose from.*

- [ ] *Work at whatever God has placed before you now instead of idly waiting for the perfect opportunity to come your way.*

Things to Remember

Lord our God, may your blessings be with us. Give us success in all we do!

PSALM 90:17 GNT

A man can't do anything better than eat and drink and be satisfied with his work. I'm finally seeing that those things also come from the hand of God.

ECCLESIASTES 2:24 NIrV

If you used to rob, you must stop robbing and start working, in order to earn an honest living for yourself and to be able to help the poor.

EPHESIANS 4:28 GNT

Then He said to His disciples, "The harvest truly is plentiful, but the laborers are few. Therefore pray the Lord of the harvest to send out laborers into His harvest."

MATTHEW 9:37–38 NKJV

Now listen, you who say, "Today or tomorrow we will go to this or that city. We will spend a year there. We will buy and sell and make money." You don't even know what will happen tomorrow. What is your life? It is a mist that appears for a little while. Then it disappears.

JAMES 4:13–14 NIrV

Make yourself indispensable, and you will move up. Act as though you are indispensable, and you will move out.

JULES ORMONT

The driving force of a career must come from the individual. Remember: Jobs are owned by the company, you own your career!

EARL NIGHTINGALE

Never-Ending Options

Trust in the LORD with all your heart, and lean not on your own understanding. In all your ways acknowledge Him, and He shall direct your paths.

—PROVERBS 3:5–6 NKJV

Of all the milestones in your life, graduation marks the time when you gain greater freedom to make your own decisions. That's not to say you didn't have to make a lot of decisions when you were in school, but now—well, life seems to consist of a never-ending stream of options. How can you expect to make all the right choices?

Accept the fact that you will make some wrong decisions. Then figure out how to reduce the number of bad choices you make, and the number of good decisions you make should outnumber the bad ones. Just as important, your wrong choices will be of the inconsequential variety, like buying a brand of toothpaste that fails to deliver that just-brushed tingle to your mouth.

How can you increase the chances that you'll make wise decisions? You can begin by taking advantage of every decision-making resource available, starting with the Word of God. Thinking of renting an apartment with someone you don't know that well? Read what the Bible says about things like relationships and trustworthiness. Can't decide which church to attend? Check out the book of Acts and the instructions given to churches in Paul's epistles to discover what kind of church life pleases God. Many Bibles include reference pages that can help you find relevant verses. In addition, there are loads of biblical resources in libraries and on the Internet, such as the Bible study tools on crosswalk.com, Biblegateway.com, and Gospelcom.net. Pray that God will give you discernment and that His Spirit will guide you toward the right decisions.

Consider all the other resources available to you: the counsel of friends and leaders; the advice of your parents; the wisdom of Christian writers whose books can help you see certain issues more clearly; and that one ever-reliable factor you might try to ignore—your gut feeling. You can probably remember a time when you went ahead and did something that turned out to be disastrous, even though you knew deep down in your gut—also known as your conscience—that it was the wrong thing to do. Don't let that happen again. Some call that gut feeling a "check in your spirit." It's a momentary hesitation that you need to pay attention to.

God has provided everything you need to make sound choices. As you mature He will add to the resources available to you—including the wisdom that He alone can give. Draw on that wisdom, and your options won't seem so daunting anymore.

I Will

Expect God to help me make the right decisions. ___ yes ___ no

Learn from the bad choices I make. ___ yes ___ no

Rely on the Word of God and His Spirit for guidance. ___ yes ___ no

Understand that the Bible has answers for the everyday decisions I have to make. ___ yes ___ no

Respond to God's leading when I sense a "check" in my spirit. ___ yes ___ no

Draw on the wisdom of God and the counsel of godly people. ___ yes ___ no

Be thankful for the many sources of help that God has placed my life. ___ yes ___ no

Things to Do

☐ *Decide right now that your first course of action will always be to consult with God.*

☐ *List the major decisions you need to make in the near future. Entrust the list to God.*

☐ *Write down the names, phone numbers, and e-mail addresses of everyone who can help you make a wise decision. Keep the list in your Bible—and use it.*

☐ *Using an online concordance, a reference work that lists every Bible verse in which a specific word is found, find the verses that will help you make the right choices.*

☐ *Think of the last time you made a bad decision and figure out what that experience taught you.*

Things to Remember

You, Lord, are all I have, and you give me all I need; my future is in your hands. How wonderful are your gifts to me; how good they are!

PSALM 16:5–6 GNT

In your heart you plan your life. But the Lord decides where your steps will take you.

PROVERBS 16:9 NIrV

Moses said to the Israelites, "I call heaven and earth as witnesses today against you, that I have set before you life and death, blessing and cursing; therefore choose life, that both you and your descendants may live."

DEUTERONOMY 30:19 NKJV

Joshua said to the Israelites, "But suppose you don't want to serve him. Then choose for yourselves right now whom you will serve. You can choose the gods your people served east of the Euphrates River. Or you can choose the gods the Amorites serve. After all, you are living in their land. But as for me and my family, we will serve the Lord."

JOSHUA 24:15 NIrV

Man's power of choice enables him to think like an angel or a devil, a king or a slave. Whatever he chooses, mind will create and manifest.

FREDERICK BAILES

Between two evils, choose neither; between two goods, choose both.

TRYON EDWARDS

Hidden in Your Heart

I will pour out My Spirit on all flesh; your sons and your daughters shall prophesy, your old men shall dream dreams, your young men shall see visions.

—JOEL 2:28 NKJV

Have you ever dreamed a really big dream—something so big that only God could make it come to pass? If not, this is a great time to start. Graduation marks your transition toward a future of unlimited opportunities—especially as you place those opportunities in the hands of your eternal Father. He wants you to trust Him to do great things through you that will bring glory and honor to His name.

Try looking at your tangible, down-to-earth plans in light of the things you tend to dream about. Maybe your primary interest has been drama, but your mind keeps wandering back to the Guatemalan children you met on a short-term mission trip. Is God leading you into mission work instead? Maybe, but maybe not. You might be the person God wants to use to create a groundbreaking type of evangelistic outreach through dramatic performances.

Or maybe you're a computer nerd but you want to make a difference in the world. You may not be able to see any way that your plans to become a Web site designer can possibly change even a small corner of the world, but if that's a dream God has placed within your heart, you can be assured He will bring it to pass.

Dreams fire your imagination. They allow you to rise above the daily bombardment of noise and words and images and enable you to catch a glimpse of the endless possibilities for your future. Dreams are what thinking outside the box is all about. They encourage you to do the unexpected, unconventional thing. Bathe them with prayer; ask God to show you why you dream about the things you do. Ask God to help you refine your dreams, and above all, ask Him to reveal to you any dream you have that is not from Him. He can see what's hidden in your heart; He knows the dreams you dream, and He will gladly destroy any that are ungodly. Don't expect Him to fulfill your dream if what you want is to be idolized by millions of people.

The Bible says that if you delight in the Lord, He will give you the desires—the dreams—of your heart. If you truly delight in the Lord, your dreams will be pleasing to Him. Go ahead—dream big dreams. Expect to do great things for God and for others. Don't limit yourself to what you see right now. Give your expectations to God—and just watch Him transform them into a reality beyond your wildest dreams.

I Will

Allow God to bring glory and honor to His name by doing great things through me.

yes _no_

Believe that God can make my productive dreams come true.

yes _no_

Learn to dream big dreams.

yes _no_

Stop dreaming about those things that are clearly not from God.

yes _no_

Bathe my hopes and aspirations in prayer.

yes _no_

Delight in the Lord.

yes _no_

Help my friends discover how God can help them achieve their dreams.

yes _no_

Things to Do

☐ _Make a list of the dreams for your life that you believe God has given you. Pray about each item._

☐ _Brainstorm with a friend about how each of you can combine your dreams with your plans._

☐ _Take one step—however small—toward making your dream come true._

☐ _Ask the Holy Spirit to reveal to you any dreams that are not of God._

☐ _Look at Goethe's quotation and dream about how you—yes, you—can move the hearts of men and women._

☐ _Thank God for allowing you to catch a glimpse of the endless possibilities He has placed in your life._

Things to Remember

The fears of the wicked will all come true; so will the hopes of the godly.

PROVERBS 10:24 NLT

Delight yourself also in the LORD, and He shall give you the desires of your heart.

PSALM 37:4 NKJV

I will give you a new heart and put a new spirit in you; I will remove from you your heart of stone and give you a heart of flesh.

EZEKIEL 36:26 NIV

The word of God is living and powerful, and sharper than any two-edged sword, piercing even to the division of soul and spirit, and of joints and marrow, and is a discerner of the thoughts and intents of the heart.

HEBREWS 4:12 NKJV

The LORD said, "Listen to my words: 'When a prophet of the LORD is among you, I reveal myself to him in visions, I speak to him in dreams.'"

NUMBERS 12:6 NIV

We all have dreams. But in order to make dreams come into reality, it takes an awful lot of determination, dedication, self-discipline, and effort.

JESSE OWENS

Dream no small dreams for they have no power to move the hearts of men.

JOHANN WOLFGANG VON GOETHE

The First Move

Godly people are careful about the friends they choose. But the way of sinners leads them down the wrong path.

—PROVERBS 12:26 NIrV

After three months at her new school, Beth had to admit that she had not made a single friend. What was wrong? She thought she was pleasant enough—no major personality disorders, gross habits, or antisocial ways. Everyone was nice to her—that wasn't the problem—but she hadn't really clicked with any of the other girls. This wasn't the way she expected college to be.

No matter which way you're heading after graduation, you may be wondering if you will find yourself to be friendless at some point. You've heard conflicting myths: "Don't worry about it. You'll have more friends than you'll know what to do with," versus "You never know whom you can trust. It's next to impossible to make new friends."

The truth lies somewhere in between. Like everyone else, you'll never have more friends than you know what to do with, and you will find people you can trust. However, a new environment can be disorienting, so you may feel nervous and a bit detached from the others at first. A new environment can also be exciting, and if you approach your new life with that attitude, you'll find it easier to relax and feel more comfortable mingling with all those strangers around you.

For any friendship to happen, someone has to make the first move. It might as well be you—but don't think you have to make a big move. Start out small. Take the initiative and introduce yourself. Invite someone out for coffee or practice hospitality in your own apartment. Get involved in an activity that would be likely to attract people with interests similar to yours: a book club, a softball team, a photography class, or any other group activity that you enjoy.

As you begin to feel more comfortable with the people around you, try starting a Bible study group related to your field of interest—creation or literature, for instance. If you're not going to continue your education, you may want to start a neighborhood Bible study using a more generic topic, such as one of the Gospels. Practice hospitality in whatever way you are able; keep it simple and casual and comfortable for everyone.

Genuine friendships take time, and deep friendships take even more time. Don't be discouraged if, like Beth, you find it more difficult to make new friends than you thought it would be. In many areas of your life, you are having to start all over again, and that includes your social life. Give yourself time to adjust; friendships will come soon enough.

I Will

Remember that friendships take time to develop. *yes* *no*

Learn to practice Christian hospitality. *yes* *no*

Entrust my social life to God. *yes* *no*

View my new life as exciting. *yes* *no*

Take the initiative in reaching out to others. *yes* *no*

Realize that I need time to adjust to my new environment. *yes* *no*

Refuse to become discouraged. *yes* *no*

Things to Do

☐ *Invite a potential friend out for coffee this week.*

☐ *Ask God to help you as you try to make new friends.*

☐ *Participate in an activity that would attract people with interests similar to yours.*

☐ *Find written or online Bible study materials that you would feel comfortable using if you decide to start a group in the future.*

☐ *Make a list of ways that you can practice hospitality, even if money is tight and space is limited.*

☐ *Think back to how you've made friends in the past and apply those principles to your present situation.*

Things to Remember

Some friendships do not last, but some friends are more loyal than brothers.

PROVERBS 18:24 GNT

I thank my God upon every remembrance of you.

PHILIPPIANS 1:3 NKJV

A friend loves at all times. He is there to help when trouble comes.

PROVERBS 17:17 NIrV

As iron sharpens iron, so one person sharpens another.

PROVERBS 27:17 NIrV

David finished talking to Saul. After that, Jonathan became David's closest friend. He loved David as much as [he loved] himself.

1 SAMUEL 18:1 GOD'S WORD

David said, "Is there still anyone who is left of the house of Saul, that I may show him kindness for Jonathan's sake?"

2 SAMUEL 9:1 NKJV

Friendship improves happiness, and abates misery, by doubling our joys, and dividing our grief.

JOSEPH ADDISON

The world is round so that friendship may encircle it.

PIERRE TEILHARD DE CHARDIN

True North

Thus speaks the LORD God of Israel, saying: "Write in a book for yourself all the words that I have spoken to you."

—JEREMIAH 30:2 NKJV

In the 1996 movie *Jerry Maguire,* the title character handles disillusionment with his job by spending all night writing a mission statement. The result is a twenty-seven-page document describing the values Maguire held when he began his career as a sports attorney and the loss of those values as he and the firm he works for became consumed with their success. Maguire ends his mission statement where his career began, with his desire to live and die for a cause—the cause of "caring about each other."

As a new graduate you have a clear advantage over Maguire, who needed to reach a crisis point before he realized how far he had strayed from the person he intended to be. You can avoid wasting years of your life—and watching your values erode—by writing a personal mission statement now, before your career gets in the way.

Just what is a mission statement? First off, it's generally not a twenty-seven-page document. It can be as short as a paragraph or as long as you want it to be. The important thing is that it defines your hopes and dreams for the kind of person you want to be and the kind of life you want to live. It's all about what's important to you, what really matters when you strip away all the inconsequential details of life.

You can write your own mission statement by simply answering a few basic questions. Here are a few:

What do you want your life to be about? As a believer you most likely would want your life to be about your relationships—first with God, and then with others. You need to answer that question for yourself, as honestly and completely as you can.

What do you want to live for? What—if anything—are you willing to die for? Think this through carefully, because your answers to these questions define exactly what your life stands for and what your values are.

What are you doing now to live the kind of life you wrote about in your previous answers? There's no need to wait until some indefinite time when you're older. If you're alive, you can start living in harmony with your mission statement right now.

The words you write can be a powerful force as long as you use them as a guiding light in your life. By regularly reviewing your mission statement, you keep reminding yourself of those things that Maguire lost sight of—the things that really matter.

I Will

Define my values and keep them in mind.   _yes_   _no_

Rely on God as I determine what my values are.   _yes_   _no_

Realize that my priority needs to be my
relationships with God and others.   _yes_   _no_

Begin living in harmony with my mission statement.   _yes_   _no_

Be honest with myself as I begin to examine what
my life is about.   _yes_   _no_

Regularly review my mission statement.   _yes_   _no_

Trust God to help me maintain my values and
standards throughout my life.   _yes_   _no_

Things to Do

☐ *Ask God to help you as you begin to write your personal mission statement.*

☐ *Find mission statements on the Internet to use as examples.*

☐ *Ask around to see if you can find an adult who has written a mission statement and is willing to help you.*

☐ *Answer the questions on the preceding page to begin writing your mission statement.*

☐ *Post your completed statement in a prominent place in your room.*

☐ *Schedule a time—say, six months or a year from now—to prayerfully review and possibly revise your statement.*

Things to Remember

In Him also we have obtained an inheritance, being predestined according to the purpose of Him who works all things according to the counsel of His will, that we who first trusted in Christ should be to the praise of His glory.

EPHESIANS 1:11–12 NKJV

God is at work with you, helping you want to obey him, and then helping you do what he wants.

PHILIPPIANS 2:13 TLB

God planned for us to do good things and to live as he has always wanted us to live. That's why he sent Christ to make us what we are.

EPHESIANS 2:10 CEV

Jesus said, "Let your light shine in front of others. Then they will see the good things you do. And they will praise your Father who is in heaven."

MATTHEW 5:16 NIrV

What you should say is this: "If the Lord is willing, we will live and do this or that."

JAMES 4:15 GNT

Above all be of single aim; have a legitimate and useful purpose, and devote yourself unreservedly to it.

JAMES ALLEN

Existence is a strange bargain. Life owes us little; we owe it everything. The only true happiness comes from squandering ourselves for a purpose.

WILLIAM COWPER

Success

Golden Opportunity

This Book of the Law shall not depart from your mouth, but you shall meditate in it day and night, that you may observe to do according to all that is written in it. For then you will make your way prosperous, and then you will have good success.

—JOSHUA 1:8 NKJV

Think of the one thing you'd like to be a success at in life. Maybe you want to be a first baseman for the New York Yankees and the proud owner of a World Series ring or two. Or your dream might be to follow in the footsteps of someone like Bill Gates and use your nerdiness to create a multibillion-dollar corporation. You might even want to be an evangelistic success and lead countless people to the Lord, the way Billy Graham and Luis Palau have.

What would it take, though, to find success in the specific area of life that appeals to you? Skill, talent, intelligence, a degree from a prestigious university, the right contacts—the luck of the draw? Many factors figure in to any successful person's journey. While your journey is in a sense just getting started, even before you graduated many of those factors were operating in your life already.

The most important one, though, is one you may not have considered, and that's your relationship with God.

Does that mean your relationship with God automatically ensures your success in the world's eyes? One look around the sanctuary on any given Sunday morning should convince you otherwise. You may see a few people who are considered a success by the community in which you live, but how many people in that community think of the word *success* when they look at the youth leader or the church secretary or the nursery workers? Yet in God's eyes those people are the success stories in His kingdom, the people who responded to Him in obedient service.

As a believer your chances of success in your chosen field are by all means better because of your relationship with God, as long as you seek His will and follow it and maintain a high degree of personal and professional integrity in your work. Just remember that God's definition of success does not always line up with that of the world's definition. Things that are important in the world's eyes—prestige, power, and wealth—are insignificant in God's eyes. He knows that the true measures of success are those things that seldom result in celebrity status, things like a heart turned fully toward Him and a deep sense of concern and compassion for the physical and spiritual well-being of others. The degree to which you serve God and others is the degree to which you will find true success in life.

I Will

Understand how God's view of success differs from the world's.

yes   no

Rely on God to make me a success in His eyes.

yes   no

Obey God and serve others.

yes   no

Seek God's will throughout my life.

yes   no

Learn to gauge my success by God's standard.

yes   no

Realize that success is a lifelong journey.

yes   no

Believe that God will direct me on the path to success.

yes   no

Things to Do

☐ Ask an older Christian what it takes to be a success.

☐ Read a book or article on success from a Christian perspective.

☐ List what you think will make you successful in your chosen field.

☐ Now pray over that list and ask God to refine it.

☐ Post either of the quotations on the next page on your mirror.

☐ Ask your parents or a friend how you've been spiritually successful so far.

☐ Read verses on success using an online Bible search.

Things to Remember

Meditate on these things; give yourself entirely to them, that your progress may be evident to all.

1 TIMOTHY 4:15 NKJV

[A wise person's] delight is in the law of the LORD, and in His law he meditates day and night. He shall be like a tree planted by the rivers of water, that brings forth its fruit in its season, whose leaf also shall not wither; and whatever he does shall prosper.

PSALM 1:2–3 NKJV

If you obey the laws and teachings that the LORD gave Moses, you will be successful. Be strong and brave and don't get discouraged or be afraid of anything.

1 CHRONICLES 22:13 CEV

Respect your father and mother, and you will live a long and successful life in the land I am giving you.

DEUTERONOMY 5:16 CEV

It is not that we think we can do anything of lasting value by ourselves. Our only power and success come from God.

2 CORINTHIANS 3:5 NLT

Size is not a measure of success. Faithfulness is a measure of success. Biblical fidelity is a measure of success.

CHARLES COLSON

It is not your business to succeed, but to do right; when you have done so, the rest lies with God.

C. S. LEWIS

Checklist for Life *for Teachers*

The end of learning is to know God, and out of that knowledge to love Him and imitate Him.

—JOHN MILTON

Smiling Before Christmas

All the days of the afflicted are evil, but he who is of a merry heart has a continual feast.

—Proverbs 15:15 NKJV

Teachers who have been in the profession for a while likely remember the advice given years ago to education majors in college: "Never smile before Christmas." The thinking at the time was that you had to maintain a stern demeanor and let your pupils know that you meant business if you expected to maintain order and discipline in the classroom. You could not drop your guard even slightly until some time halfway through the school year, when the students were so used to your strictness that you could afford to smile now and then.

What were those professors thinking? Imagine all of those bright young college students, full of eagerness to teach and affection for children, suddenly being told that they had to ignore their instincts in order to lay down the law. Imagine *you* being told that today. Thankfully, that piece of advice went the way of corporal punishment in the classroom as educational researchers began to realize that children learned best in a loving, nurturing, and cheerful environment. Teachers, of course, knew all along that it's nearly impossible to suppress a smile when you're surrounded all day by some of the funniest and most charming people on the planet, no matter how exasperating they may be at times.

So smile—and keep smiling. Your cheerfulness in the classroom can turn a bad day around for the boy whose home life is in shambles, the girl whose grades are causing her stress, and every other student who just needs to see a smiling face, for whatever reason. And the great thing about it is that you can *decide* to be cheerful, regardless of the circumstances in your own life or the kind of day you are having. Choosing to be cheerful is not a form of deception, either. By *acting* cheerful, you can actually *become* cheerful. You simply set your own problems aside temporarily, resolving to deal with them when you're away from the watchful eyes of the young people who need you to bring a bit of sunshine into their lives.

The Bible says that God loves a cheerful giver. That verse applies to money, but it's probably safe to assume that He's equally pleased when you cheerfully give of yourself in the classroom. Ask Him to help you light up that room by maintaining a pleasant countenance and attitude throughout the day. Put a smile on your face—before, during, and after Christmas.

I Will

Decide to be cheerful.   yes ___   no ___

Realize that my countenance affects my students.   yes ___   no ___

Smile before Christmas.   yes ___   no ___

Thank God for the delightful young people He has
placed in my life.   yes ___   no ___

Set aside my own problems when I'm in the
presence of my students.   yes ___   no ___

Pray that I will be able to bring some sunshine
into others' lives.   yes ___   no ___

Remember to maintain a cheerful attitude around
my colleagues as well.   yes ___   no ___

Things to Do

☐ Memorize one of the accompanying Scriptures so you can recall it during the school day.

☐ Place a rubber band around your wrist for one day and snap it—hard—each time you catch yourself acting gloomy; see how quickly you cheer up.

☐ Decorate your classroom to create a sunny, cheerful environment.

☐ Come up with a variety of pleasant responses to unpleasant remarks you're likely to hear at school.

☐ Make a list of the ways you can be more cheerful as a teacher and do the first three immediately (for example, stand by the door and greet students by name as they enter the room—even in high school).

☐ Start a collection of uplifting quotations to use in lessons or post in your classroom.

Things to Remember

Always look happy and cheerful.

ECCLESIASTES 9:8 GNT

Let each one give as he has planned in his heart, neither grudgingly nor by compulsion; for God loves a happy giver.

2 CORINTHIANS 9:7 MLB

Are any of you in trouble? Then you should pray. Are any of you happy? Then sing songs of praise.

JAMES 5:13 NIrV

A joyful heart makes a cheerful face, but when the heart is sad, the spirit is broken.

PROVERBS 15:13 NASB

David wrote, "When I was upset and beside myself, you calmed me down and cheered me up."

PSALM 94:19 THE MESSAGE

Happy are the people who are in such a state; happy are the people whose God is the LORD!

PSALM 144:15 NKJV

It is not fitting, when one is in God's service, to have a gloomy face or a chilling look.
—SAINT FRANCIS OF ASSISI

Let us be of good cheer, knowing that the misfortunes hardest to bear are those which never happen.
—JAMES RUSSELL LOWELL

Goals

Multiple Choice

One thing I do, forgetting those things which are behind and reaching forward to those things which are ahead, I press toward the goal for the prize of the upward call of God in Christ Jesus.

—PHILIPPIANS 3:13–14 NKJV

You already know what it takes to meet a goal in your life. You wanted to be a teacher, and you accomplished that goal. Now, with myriad responsibilities and challenges vying for your attention, you may have this nagging awareness in the back of your mind that you should continue to set goals for your life, but there never seems to be enough time to give goal-setting the attention it deserves.

If that's the case, start small. Jot down things you'd like to do, whenever the thought occurs to you; a small, palm-sized voice recorder is great for something like this. Don't restrict yourself to professional goals. Maybe you want to learn to fly or do an in-depth study of the book of Revelation. Write down and record everything.

When you have a few minutes, pick just one item on your list. Say you've always wanted to go back to school and earn a master's in education, but you don't want to relocate and uproot your children, and you don't know how your family would survive without your income anyway. Take that one item and do just one activity related to that goal. For example, do some online research. You may discover that the very school you wish to attend now offers a distance learning program that would allow you to earn most of your credits online, and that the site has links to numerous organizations that offer grants to teachers who want to continue their education.

If you keep taking incremental steps like that toward each of your goals, you'll be on your way toward earning your pilot's license and mastering the book of Revelation in no time. Sometimes the enormity of an accomplishment is all it takes to discourage people from pursuing their passions in life. But once you get in the habit of turning each desire into an achievable goal and breaking that goal into smaller steps, your aspirations shrink to manageable proportions.

So go ahead—dream big. Invite God into the process and ask Him to help you refine your goals and bring them into line with His will. Pray about them every step of the way. Keep track of your progress; little by little you'll realize that you are actually getting closer to the goal line. Once you reach a goal, remember to celebrate. And while you're at it, remember to thank God and anyone else who helped you along the way.

I Will

Ask God to help me set achievable goals for
my life.   *yes*   *no*

Break larger goals down into smaller steps to
avoid frustration.   *yes*   *no*

Express my gratitude to everyone who helped me
achieve my aspirations.   *yes*   *no*

Celebrate each time I meet a goal in my life.   *yes*   *no*

Dream big.   *yes*   *no*

Appreciate all that I've already accomplished.   *yes*   *no*

Refuse to become discouraged when my goals
seem unattainable.   *yes*   *no*

Things to Do

☐ *Start a list of goals for your life—personal, spiritual, and professional.*

☐ *Read Philippians 3:7–21, in which Paul describes his aspirations and encourages believers to have similar goals.*

☐ *Look over the next big project you'll be assigning, and make sure you break it down into smaller steps for your students.*

☐ *Choose a goal you've had in mind for a long time and consider the reasons why you haven't achieved it—and how that's going to change.*

☐ *Set aside some time this week—even if it's only fifteen minutes or so—to work on just one of your goals.*

☐ *Seek the prayer support of several people as you strive to meet one of your more difficult goals.*

Things to Remember

Everyone who competes for the prize is temperate in all things. Now they do it to obtain a perishable crown, but we for an imperishable crown.

1 CORINTHIANS 9:25 NKJV

Looking unto Jesus, the author and finisher of our faith, who for the joy that was set before Him endured the cross, despising the shame, and has sat down at the right hand of the throne of God.

HEBREWS 12:2 NKJV

As long, then, as that promise of resting in him pulls us on to God's goal for us, we need to be careful that we're not disqualified.

HEBREWS 4:1 THE MESSAGE

I have not yet reached my goal, and I am not perfect. But Christ has taken hold of me. So I keep on running and struggling to take hold of the prize.

PHILIPPIANS 3:12 CEV

The vision will still happen at the appointed time. It hurries toward its goal. It won't be a lie. If it's delayed, wait for it. It will certainly happen. It won't be late.

HABAKKUK 2:3 GOD'S WORD

No one can be making much of his life who has not a very definite conception of what he is living for.

—WASHINGTON IRVING

It's kind of fun to do the impossible.

—WALT DISNEY

Time Management

After Hours

Walk circumspectly, not as fools but as wise, redeeming the time, because the days are evil.

—EPHESIANS 5:15–16 NKJV

Mrs. Geller's job as a middle-school English instructor required more work than she could possibly expect to get done on the clock. She had a full—no, an overflowing—plate. Waking up before dawn, she filled her day with tutoring, thinking of ways to keep her classes interesting, grading tests and homework, and attempting to find a few moments of peace in between the rush of adolescent children entering and exiting her room.

After school, Mrs. Geller had to pick up her own children from daycare, get any necessary shopping done, attempt to prepare a nutritious dinner, tidy up the house, and spend time with her family. That usually left about fifteen good minutes to finish grading papers before she collapsed into bed.

Like many teachers, Mrs. Geller rarely finished the things she set out to do in a single day. She knew her students viewed her as an "easy" teacher; it was difficult to expect her students to adhere to deadlines when she couldn't. Plus, she felt she was missing out on precious time with her own children. But with her full workload, she had no time to work out a solution.

Then, one January morning, school was canceled due to a snowstorm. In her typical "must get everything done" frame of mind, she used the time to catch up on grading papers, planning next week's lessons, and doing the laundry. To her surprise, by midafternoon she had nothing urgent left to do. She invited a snow-shoveling neighbor in for a hot cup of coffee and spent a treasured, quiet evening with her family.

At the end of her surprise vacation day, Mrs. Geller realized what a burden her busy schedule had become. In her frenzy to get everything done—a feat no one ever accomplishes—she had been working against time rather than with it. The following Saturday morning, she sat down with her husband and worked out a schedule for managing the daily work of running a household. That afternoon, she spent three uninterrupted hours brainstorming about ways she could streamline her work-related tasks and manage her workload more efficiently.

The Bible tells you not to worry about tomorrow, but sometimes it is difficult to keep that in mind when life demands that you do twenty-four hours worth of tasks in eighteen hours. But few people benefit from a frantic schedule. On the contrary, most people suffer, along with everyone around them. Bring God into your schedule planning; He invented time, and He can help you manage it. When you come up with a reasonable schedule—and stick to it as much as possible—the pressure eases up, and you are far more likely to accomplish what you set out to do.

I Will

Work *with* time instead of *against* it.   yes   no

Take the time to come up with solutions to my
time management problems.   yes   no

Realize that no one ever gets everything done;
there will always be something else to do.   yes   no

Ask God to help me create a realistic schedule
for my personal and professional life.   yes   no

Guard against the habit of racing through life
at a frantic pace.   yes   no

Take full advantage of God-sent breaks and
blessings, like an unexpected day off.   yes   no

Things to Do

☐ *Use your computer to save time by creating templates of frequently used forms and documents.*

☐ *Go through your lesson plan book and schedule time for planning, paperwork, and work-related reading (including professional development materials).*

☐ *Search online for sites that offer lesson plans that you can use when you're pressed for time.*

☐ *Ask for parents' e-mail addresses and create a group listing in your address book for sending notices home. Print out messages for students without e-mail.*

☐ *Call a family meeting to create a manageable schedule for chores and relaxation.*

Things to Remember

Remember now Your Creator in the days of your youth, before the difficult days come, and the years draw near when you say, "I have no pleasure in them."

ECCLESIASTES 12:1 NKJV

To everything there is a season, a time for every purpose under heaven.

ECCLESIASTES 3:1 NKJV

He who keeps his command will experience nothing harmful; and a wise man's heart discerns both time and judgment.

ECCLESIASTES 8:5 NKJV

A thousand years in Your sight are like yesterday when it is past, and like a watch in the night.

PSALM 90:4 NKJV

Mordecai said to Esther, "If you remain silent at this time, relief and deliverance will arise for the Jews from another place and you and your father's house will perish. And who knows whether you have not attained royalty for such a time as this?"

ESTHER 4:14 NASB

God says, "At just the right time, I heard you. On the day of salvation, I helped you." Indeed, God is ready to help you right now. Today is the day of salvation.

2 CORINTHIANS 6:2 NLT

How you spend your time is more important than how you spend your money. Money mistakes can be corrected, but time is gone forever.

—DAVID B. NORRIS

Half our life is spent trying to find something to do with the time we have rushed through life trying to save.

—WILL ROGERS

Praise

Raising Your Voice

Praise the Lord! Praise the Lord, O my soul! While I live I will praise the Lord; I will sing praises to my God while I have my being.

—Psalm 146:1–2 NKJV

At the start of the summer following his first year of teaching, Adam Walker had some serious thinking to do. The school year had been uneven at best—lots of highs, lots of lows, but mostly lots of nights questioning his suitability for the teaching profession. The son of two teachers, Adam considered himself better prepared for the challenges of teaching than most education majors he had met in college. But he wasn't prepared for the gradual erosion of his relationship with God during long and hectic days that too frequently had left him discouraged.

Before starting a summer job, Adam spent a much-needed week with his parents. As he had anticipated, these two veterans of a combined half century in the classroom listened to their son's concerns, asked questions, prayed with him and without him, offered theories about why he was discouraged, and listened some more. Of all the suggestions they made, there was one he could work on over the summer—praising God throughout the day. As

Adam's father had pointed out, his understanding of praise was incomplete; the only time he praised God was when things were going well. He had confused praise with thankfulness.

As Adam learned, God wants His people to praise Him no matter what happens, as David wrote in Psalm 34:1. In fact, David, who had a lifetime of opportunities to become discouraged and feel alienated from God, discovered the value of praising God and left a wealth of wisdom regarding praise in the many psalms he wrote. He pledged to praise God "every day . . . forever and ever" (Psalm 145:2 NKJV), "with my whole heart" (Psalm 138:1 NKJV). He praised God for who He is and not just for His works; he praised God even when the tide had turned against him.

When you immerse yourself in the book of Psalms, you discover the value of praising God all the time, in a variety of ways and circumstances, whether you feel like it or not. Praising God can readily become a habit in your life, one that you can practice throughout the day, no matter where you are. Whether you express yourself verbally, silently, in song, on paper, in your work or in your play, alone or with others, God is waiting for you to praise Him with your whole heart.

I Will

Realize that God wants me to praise Him.
yes no

Remember to praise God for who He is and not
just what He has done for me.
yes no

Praise God for everything, whether good or bad.
yes no

Learn how to praise God in different and creative
ways: silently, vocally, through singing and writing,
and so forth.
yes no

Ask God to give me a heart of praise.
yes no

Praise God even when I don't feel like it.
yes no

Realize that nature also praises God
(Luke 19:37–40).
yes no

Things to Do

☐ *Look up synonyms for the verb form of* praise *in a thesaurus or at www.dictionary.com and select a half dozen or so—such as glorify, bless, worship—to use in your praise of God.*

☐ *Schedule several praise breaks—even a minute of praising God will help—throughout each school day this week.*

☐ *Choose several "praise" psalms—such as Psalms 9, 22, 30, 71—and pray them aloud to God.*

☐ *Try to write your own psalms of praise to the Lord.*

☐ *Visit a church radically different from your own and observe how the people praise God.*

☐ *Sing a song of praise to God—even if you "can't" sing.*

Things to Remember

All together now—applause for God!
Sing songs to the tune of his glory, set
glory to the rhythms of his praise!

PSALM 66:1–2 THE MESSAGE

I proclaim the name of the LORD:
Ascribe greatness to our God.

DEUTERONOMY 32:3 NKJV

Sing to Him, sing psalms to Him; talk of
all His wondrous works!

PSALM 105:2 NKJV

Praise the LORD from the heavens; praise
Him in the heights! Praise Him, all His
angels; praise Him, all His hosts! Praise
Him, sun and moon; praise Him, all
you stars of light!

PSALM 148:1–3 NKJV

I will praise the LORD no matter what
happens. I will constantly speak of his
glories and grace.

PSALM 34:1 TLB

O LORD, I will praise you with all my
heart, and tell everyone about the
marvelous things you do.

PSALM 9:1 TLB

**To say "well done"
to any bit of good
work is to take
hold of the powers
which have made
the effort and
strengthen them
beyond our
knowledge.**

—PHILLIPS BROOKS

**We increase
whatever we praise.
The whole creation
responds to praise,
and is glad.**

—CHARLES FILLMORE

Celebration

Party Time

They will talk together about the glory of your kingdom; they will celebrate examples of your power.

—Psalm 145:11 NLT

Party people—they're in every school. They're the teachers or the administrators who organize the monthly parties for all those who are celebrating their birthdays that month. They're the ones who know that Mrs. Christopher likes white cake with strawberry icing, Principal Adams prefers German chocolate cake with walnuts, and Mr. Griffin simply has to have red velvet cake with cream cheese icing—and they all celebrate their birthdays in the same month. What on earth will the party people do now?

There's no need for a celebration to be so complicated. There's not even any need for a celebration to be tied to a special occasion like a birthday. Is the sun shining after two whole weeks of cold and rainy weather? That certainly calls for a celebration. But even better are the celebrations that acknowledge the little victories that often go unnoticed in people's lives. A teacher who's been waiting for the results of some frightening medical tests deserves a treat when the results come back negative. A child whose father returns home after fighting in a war overseas could stand a bit of celebrating. And you—don't forget yourself. You need to remember to celebrate, even when no one but you knows about your victories.

The most important element in any celebration is not the food or the decorations, the location or even the occasion itself. The most important element is the people. A simple celebration honoring a coworker who reached tenure, or had an article published in a prestigious education journal, or finally got approval to use the curriculum of her choosing makes the person realize that someone *noticed*, someone paid attention and realized that something important had happened, no matter how minor it may seem to other people.

There's simply no substitute for being attentive to others. When you really pay attention to other people and congratulate them on a little-known accomplishment, they're often stunned to realize that you are aware of what's going on in their lives. Imagine if you called for a celebration! Go ahead and do it, even if the celebration consists of a cup of coffee at a café down the street.

People all around you are starved for genuine, caring attention. By celebrating the big and little milestones in their lives, you show them just how important they are to you—and that often opens the door to showing them just how important they are to God. Go ahead—celebrate! The angels in heaven are rejoicing right along with you.

I Will

Give myself permission to have fun and enjoy life.   *yes* ___   *no* ___

Be on the lookout for milestones and occasions for celebration.   *yes* ___   *no* ___

Be aware of any tendency I may have to take life too seriously.   *yes* ___   *no* ___

Realize that God wants to be a part of my times of celebration.   *yes* ___   *no* ___

Rediscover the joy of spontaneous fun.   *yes* ___   *no* ___

Thank God for the many sources of pleasure He has provided.   *yes* ___   *no* ___

Share my enthusiasm for life with others.   *yes* ___   *no* ___

Things to Do

☐ *Celebrate the next unusual "national" day—like National Pickle Day—in an appropriately fun way in your classroom.*

☐ *Come up with a way to celebrate the little things that happen to your students, especially those who seldom receive academic or popular recognition.*

☐ *Plan an end-of-the-school-year celebration with several other teachers.*

☐ *Celebrate your relationship with God by spending an entire day alone with Him.*

☐ *Treat a friend who does not know God to a special event, such as a concert or play or sports competition, just for the fun of it.*

☐ *List as many things as you can think of that you love to do—even things you haven't done in years—and start doing them again.*

Things to Remember

A voice came from the throne, saying, "Praise our God, all you His servants and those who fear Him, both small and great!"

REVELATION 19:5 NKJV

Young women will dance and be glad. And so will the men, young and old alike. I will turn their sobbing into gladness. I will comfort them. And I will give them joy instead of sorrow.

JEREMIAH 31:13 NIrV

Jesus said, "Count on it—that's the kind of party God's angels throw every time one lost soul turns to God."

LUKE 15:10 THE MESSAGE

The ransomed of the LORD shall return, and come to Zion with singing, with everlasting joy on their heads. They shall obtain joy and gladness, and sorrow and sighing shall flee away.

ISAIAH 35:10 NKJV

Neighbors ranging from as far north as Issachar, Zebulun, and Naphtali arrived with donkeys, camels, mules, and oxen loaded down with food for the party: flour, fig cakes, raisin cakes, wine, oil, cattle, and sheep—joy in Israel!

1 CHRONICLES 12:40 THE MESSAGE

Celebrate what you want to see more of.

—THOMAS J. PETERS

We have all eternity to celebrate our victories, but only one short hour before sunset in which to win them.

—ROBERT MOFFAT

Scripture Translations Used in *The Ultimate Checklist for Life*